Police
Brutality

OPPOSING VIEWPOINTS®

Police
Brutality

OPPOSING VIEWPOINTS®

Other Books of Related Interest

Police Brutality

OPPOSING VIEWPOINTS®

Helen Cothran, *Book Editor*

David L. Bender, *Publisher*
Bruno Leone, *Executive Editor*
Bonnie Szumski, *Editorial Director*
Stuart B. Miller, *Managing Editor*

OPPOSING
VIEWPOINTS®
SERIES

Greenhaven Press, Inc., San Diego, California

NOV 2 7 2000

Cover photo: © Corbis

Library of Congress Cataloging-in-Publication Data

Police brutality : opposing viewpoints / Helen Cothran, book editor.
    p.   cm. — (Opposing viewpoints series)
  Includes bibliographical references and index.
  ISBN 0-7377-0516-7 (lib. bdg. : alk. paper) —
ISBN 0-7377-0515-9 (pbk. : alk. paper)
  1. Police brutality—United States. 2. Discrimination in law
enforcement—United States. 3. Police—Complaints against—
United States. 4. Police-community relations—United States.
I. Cothran, Helen. II. Opposing viewpoints series (Unnumbered)

HV8141 .P57 2001
363.2'32—dc21   00-032996
                                                        CIP

Greenhaven Press, Inc., P.O. Box 289009
San Diego, CA 92198-9009

"Congress shall make
no law...abridging the
freedom of speech, or of
the press."

First Amendment to the U.S. Constitution

The basic foundation of our democracy is the First
Amendment guarantee of freedom of expression. The
Opposing Viewpoints Series is dedicated to the
concept of this basic freedom and the idea that it is
more important to practice it than to enshrine it.

Contents

Why Consider Opposing Viewpoints?

"The only way in which a human being can make some approach to knowing the whole of a subject is by hearing what can be said about it by persons of every variety of opinion and studying all modes in which it can be looked at by every character of mind. No wise man ever acquired his wisdom in any mode but this."

John Stuart Mill

In our media-intensive culture it is not difficult to find differing opinions. Thousands of newspapers and magazines and dozens of radio and television talk shows resound with differing points of view. The difficulty lies in deciding which opinion to agree with and which "experts" seem the most credible. The more inundated we become with differing opinions and claims, the more essential it is to hone critical reading and thinking skills to evaluate these ideas. Opposing Viewpoints books address this problem directly by presenting stimulating debates that can be used to enhance and teach these skills. The varied opinions contained in each book examine many different aspects of a single issue. While examining these conveniently edited opposing views, readers can develop critical thinking skills such as the ability to compare and contrast authors' credibility, facts, argumentation styles, use of persuasive techniques, and other stylistic tools. In short, the Opposing Viewpoints Series is an ideal way to attain the higher-level thinking and reading skills so essential in a culture of diverse and contradictory opinions.

In addition to providing a tool for critical thinking, Opposing Viewpoints books challenge readers to question their own strongly held opinions and assumptions. Most people form their opinions on the basis of upbringing, peer pressure, and personal, cultural, or professional bias. By reading carefully balanced opposing views, readers must directly confront new ideas as well as the opinions of those with whom they disagree. This is not to simplistically argue that everyone who reads opposing views will—or should—change his or her opinion. Instead, the series enhances readers' understanding of their own views by encouraging confrontation with opposing ideas. Careful examination of others' views can lead to the readers' understanding of the logical inconsistencies in their own opinions, perspective on why they hold an opinion, and the consideration of the possibility that their opinion requires further evaluation.

Evaluating Other Opinions

To ensure that this type of examination occurs, Opposing Viewpoints books present all types of opinions. Prominent spokespeople on different sides of each issue as well as well-known professionals from many disciplines challenge the reader. An additional goal of the series is to provide a forum for other, less known, or even unpopular viewpoints. The opinion of an ordinary person who has had to make the decision to cut off life support from a terminally ill relative, for example, may be just as valuable and provide just as much insight as a medical ethicist's professional opinion. The editors have two additional purposes in including these less known views. One, the editors encourage readers to respect others' opinions—even when not enhanced by professional credibility. It is only by reading or listening to and objectively evaluating others' ideas that one can determine whether they are worthy of consideration. Two, the inclusion of such viewpoints encourages the important critical thinking skill of objectively evaluating an author's credentials and bias. This evaluation will illuminate an author's reasons for taking a particular stance on an issue and will aid in readers' evaluation of the author's ideas.

As series editors of the Opposing Viewpoints Series, it is our hope that these books will give readers a deeper understanding of the issues debated and an appreciation of the complexity of even seemingly simple issues when good and honest people disagree. This awareness is particularly important in a democratic society such as ours in which people enter into public debate to determine the common good.

Those with whom one disagrees should not be regarded as enemies but rather as people whose views deserve careful examination and may shed light on one's own.

Thomas Jefferson once said that "difference of opinion leads to inquiry, and inquiry to truth." Jefferson, a broadly educated man, argued that "if a nation expects to be ignorant and free . . . it expects what never was and never will be." As individuals and as a nation, it is imperative that we consider the opinions of others and examine them with skill and discernment. The Opposing Viewpoints Series is intended to help readers achieve this goal.

David L. Bender & Bruno Leone,
Series Editors

Greenhaven Press anthologies primarily consist of previously published material taken from a variety of sources, including periodicals, books, scholarly journals, newspapers, government documents, and position papers from private and public organizations. These original sources are often edited for length and to ensure their accessibility for a young adult audience. The anthology editors also change the original titles of these works in order to clearly present the main thesis of each viewpoint and to explicitly indicate the opinion presented in the viewpoint. These alterations are made in consideration of both the reading and comprehension levels of a young adult audience. Every effort is made to ensure that Greenhaven Press accurately reflects the original intent of the authors included in this anthology.

Introduction

"Police don't respect the rights of young people."
  —*Richie Perez, National Congress for Puerto Rican Rights*

*"We're not out there to antagonize or oppress, we're out
  there to maintain the peace."*
                    —*Dennis Fitzgerald, New York City police officer*

One summer night in 1995 in New York City, teenager
Rance Scully and three of his friends were walking home
from a party when they noticed a police car following them.
The four teenagers were doing nothing wrong, so Scully
convinced his friends that they should turn around and go
talk with the officers. When they headed for the patrol car,
the officers suddenly blinded them with a police light and
ordered them to stop and spread their legs. Three cops
jumped out of the car with guns drawn and surrounded the
frightened teens. After aggressively interrogating and searching Scully and his friends, the police released them.

In New York City, police arrested two teenage boys and a
young woman who repeatedly raped and tortured a thirteen-
year-old girl, and then hung her up in a closet; fortunately,
the girl escaped. A five-year-old in Chicago was not so lucky.
Two boys—one twelve, the other thirteen—were arrested
and convicted of dropping him out of a fourteenth-story window, killing him.

Teens and young adults are increasingly involved in encounters with police. The frightening ordeal experienced by
Scully and his friends can cause many young people to fear
law enforcement, yet police contend that they need to monitor teens more closely due to the brutal nature of some
crimes committed by teens.

Teen-police conflicts are escalating as teen crime rates
rise. According to the Heritage Foundation, teenagers are
responsible for most of the violent crimes in the United
States. In response to the high incidence of teen crime, police often increase their presence where crime occurs. For
example, New York City mayor Rudolph Giuliani ordered

the New York City Police Department to control security at the city's schools after several shootings by teens occurred on school grounds. Another example of stronger police presence can be seen in the creation of gang-control units that patrol the streets on a regular basis. Since up to 90 percent of gang members are juveniles, run-ins between police in gang-control units and teens are increasingly common.

Many teenagers argue, however, that they are being unfairly harassed and brutalized by law enforcement just because some teens commit violent crimes. Alex Stephen, sixteen, of New York City, said her cousin was beaten by police officers in 1989. Nagib Nabi, seventeen, claims that New York City police stopped and frisked him even though he had not done anything wrong. "They tried to intimidate me by calling me 'sp-c' and other insulting names," he contends. "And they threw me on the wall, and as I turned around they hit me with the baton on the back of my head." Gia Minetta, another teen from New York City, claims that during a police sweep, officers "grabbed my arm, twisted it behind me . . . and threw me up against the police van." According to Minetta, she and her friends had done nothing to provoke the brutal treatment by police.

Statistics show that police are focusing more on teens and juvenile crime. Kim Nauer, a writer for *City Limits*, reports that in New York City juvenile arrests jumped almost 30 percent in the first year under Mayor Giuliani. In 1984, she claims, "police arrested 98,413 children and teenagers on everything from loitering to murder." Almost half of those arrests were for "non-fingerprintable offenses," meaning minor crimes like public drinking or disorderly conduct. Community activists who want to protect teens from police harassment protest the extent of those arrests. Joyce Hall, executive director of the Greater Brownsville Youth Council in New York City, claims that the arrests create a "cycle" in which teens who feel that they are treated disrespectfully by police "lash back, getting themselves into even deeper trouble with the law."

But police see the teen crime situation very differently. More than one-third of all murders are committed by offenders under the age of twenty-one, guns are used in juvenile crimes at almost twice the rate they were in 1984, and teen drug and alcohol use—factors that contribute to juvenile crime—are on the rise. In 1995, nearly 11 percent of juveniles admitted to using illicit drugs; in the period between 1995 and 1996, 31 percent of twelfth-graders admitted to consuming alcohol to get drunk. These statistics raise legitimate concerns about teen criminality, police assert; therefore, they maintain that they are justified in closely watching teens for trouble in order to reduce crime. New York City police commissioner William Bratton argues that arresting teens for minor crimes such as subway turnstile–jumping will prevent more serious crimes because weapons and drugs are often found on these youths; confiscating the drugs and weapons can prevent teens from using them and committing future crimes.

Police officers, like teens, also feel that they are stereotyped and misunderstood. Officer Beverly Riggins from the New York City Police Department argues that "teens have negative ideas [about cops] based on television programs; our jobs are nowhere near what television portrays." Retired police lieutenant Arthur Doyle asserts that teens develop stereotypes about police just as police do about teens. If a young man sees a friend harassed by an abusive cop, for example, he will tend to view all police officers as abusive.

In many ways, police-teen conflicts mirror the conflicts any civilian might have with police. Adults, like teens, sometimes claim that police harass them and discriminate against them. Police respond to these charges with statistics about crime rates and explanations about the dangerous nature of police work. The issue of discrimination is central to the debate surrounding police brutality. The contributors to *Police Brutality: Opposing Viewpoints* address this and other questions surrounding police brutality in the following chapters: Is Misconduct by Law Enforcement a Serious Problem? What Factors Cause Police Brutality? Do Modern Police Methods Cause Police Misconduct? Who Should Police the Police? When examining the viewpoints in this book, it becomes clear that the relationship between police and those they serve is an important issue in discussions about police brutality.

CHAPTER 1

Is Misconduct by Law Enforcement a Serious Problem?

Chapter Preface

In late 1992, the Bureau of Alcohol, Tobacco, and Firearms (ATF) received information that the Branch Davidian cult in Waco, Texas, was collecting illegal firearms. When the ATF agents arrived at the Davidian compound with a search warrant in February 1993, the cult's leader, David Koresh, would not comply, and the Davidians opened fire. Six cult members and four ATF agents were killed.

After the failed ATF raid, the FBI took over and for fifty-one days tried several tactics to drive the cult members out of the compound. On the morning of April 19, FBI agents began using tanks to punch holes in the walls of the buildings, and agents inserted tear gas into the compound. Soon after, the buildings went up in flames. When federal agents entered the burned compound, they found that over eighty members of the cult—twenty-four of whom were children—had died.

Much controversy surrounds the FBI's actions during the Waco siege. Defenders of the FBI's operation argue that the FBI was justified in using aggressive action against the cult, reasoning that if the Davidians had not posed a threat to society they would have complied with a search warrant. Edwin O. Guthman, an investigator into the government's role in the Waco tragedy, defended the agents' actions by saying, "it seems quite clear [the Davidians] were given every opportunity to come out, to save the lives of other people there, and that didn't happen."

Critics of the FBI's operation maintain that the Davidians posed no threat and claim that the actions against them were brutal and incompetent. They also argue that the FBI covered up instances of wrongdoing by agents during the siege. Paul Greenberg, editorial editor of the *Arkansas Democrat-Gazette*, called the Waco operation a "monstrous blunder."

Federal investigations into the Waco siege six years after the fact have not resolved the issue of whether the FBI's actions were justifiable. Determining if police action against civilians is justified can be made difficult by personal and political ideology. The question of whether or not misconduct by law enforcement represents a serious problem is debated in the following chapter.

"Police abuse remains one of the most serious and divisive human rights violations in the United States."

Police Brutality Is a Serious Problem

Human Rights Watch

Human Rights Watch is an international organization that monitors abuses of human rights. In the following viewpoint, the organization contends that police brutality is pervasive in the United States because police are granted the power to use deadly force and face little accountability for their actions. According to Human Rights Watch, to reduce or prevent police brutality, law enforcement officers must be subjected to intense scrutiny by local, federal, and international authorities.

As you read, consider the following questions:
1. What reforms did the Justice Department recommend to Pittsburgh and Steubenville, according to Human Rights Watch?
2. According to the organization, what is the definition of a "problem officer"?
3. How many police officers died while on duty in the United States in 1996, according to the organization?

Excerpted from the overview of the 1998 report "Shielded from Justice: Police Brutality and Accountability in the United States," published by the Human Rights Watch at www.hrw.org/reports98/police/uspol4.htm. Reprinted with permission. Endnotes in the original have been omitted in this reprint.

P olice abuse remains one of the most serious and divisive human rights violations in the United States. The excessive use of force by police officers, including unjustified shootings, severe beatings, fatal chokings, and rough treatment, persists because overwhelming barriers to accountability make it possible for officers who commit human rights violations to escape due punishment and often to repeat their offenses. Police or public officials greet each new report of brutality with denials or explain that the act was an aberration, while the administrative and criminal systems that should deter these abuses by holding officers accountable instead virtually guarantee them impunity. . . .

Widespread Brutality

This report examines common obstacles to accountability for police abuse in fourteen large cities representing most regions of the nation. The cities examined are: Atlanta, Boston, Chicago, Detroit, Indianapolis, Los Angeles, Minneapolis, New Orleans, New York, Philadelphia, Portland, Providence, San Francisco, and Washington, D.C. Research for this report was conducted over two and a half years, from late 1995 through early 1998. . . .

It is important to note . . . that because it is difficult to obtain case information except where there is public scandal and/or prosecution, this viewpoint relies heavily on cases that have reached public attention; disciplinary action and criminal prosecution are even less common than the cases set out below would suggest.

Our investigation found that police brutality is persistent in all of these cities; that systems to deal with abuse have had similar failings in all the cities; and that, in each city examined, complainants face enormous barriers in seeking administrative punishment or criminal prosecution of officers who have committed human rights violations. Despite claims to the contrary from city officials where abuses have become scandals in the media, efforts to make meaningful reforms have fallen short.

Barriers to Accountability

The barriers to accountability are remarkably similar from city to city. Shortcomings in recruitment, training, and management are common to all. So is the fact that officers who repeatedly commit human rights violations tend to be a small minority who taint entire police departments but are protected, routinely, by the silence of their fellow officers and by flawed systems of reporting, oversight, and accountability. Another pervasive shortcoming is the scarcity of meaningful information about trends in abuse; data are also lacking regarding the police departments' response to those incidents and their plans or actions to prevent brutality. Where data do exist, there is no evidence that police administrators or, where relevant, prosecutors, utilize available information in a way to deter abuse. Another commonality in recent years is a recognition, in most cities, about what needs to be done to fix troubled departments. However, this encouraging development is coupled with an official unwillingness to deal seriously with officers who commit abuses until high-profile cases expose long-standing negligence or tolerance of brutality.

One recent, positive development has been the federal "pattern or practice" civil investigations, and subsequent agreements, initiated by the U.S. Justice Department. In Pittsburgh, Pennsylvania, and Steubenville, Ohio, the Justice Department's Civil Rights Division has examined shortcomings in accountability for misconduct in those cities' police departments; the cities agreed to implement reforms to end violative practices rather than risk the Justice Department taking a case to court for injunctive action. The reforms proposed by the Justice Department were similar to those long advocated by community activists and civil rights groups, and included better use-of-force training and policies, stronger reporting mechanisms, creation of early warning systems to identify current, and potential, officers at risk of engaging in abuse, and improved disciplinary procedures. The Justice Department does not usually make its investigative choices public, but several other police departments, including those in Los Angeles, New Orleans, New York, and Philadelphia, are reportedly under investigation by the Civil Rights Division.

Problem Officers

Police abuse experts, and some police officials, refer to "problem" officers, by which they mean officers who either have significant records of abuse or significant records of complaints from the public, and who thus should receive special monitoring, training, and counseling to counter the heightened risk that they will be involved in some future incident of misconduct or brutality. In this report, we will use this terminology where police officials and experts use it, to denote officers who, on account of their record of either sustained or unsustained complaints, appear to present a higher than normal risk of committing human rights violations.

Britt. Reprinted by permission of Copley News Service.

Allegations of police abuse are rife in cities throughout the country and take many forms. This report uses specific incidents as illustrations of the obstacles to deterring, investigating, and acting upon perceived abuses. Human Rights Watch is presenting these cases *not* to accuse any particular officer of an abuse, but rather to describe the barriers that exist to addressing such allegations meaningfully. Any alleged abuse has a corrosive effect on public trust of the police force, and it is imperative that the system be reformed to prevent human rights violations such as those described below.

An Example of Abuse

• A seriously flawed background check of a new recruit who had a history of abusive behavior while working for another police department, apparent misuse of pepper spray, and poor investigation procedures were evident in the Aaron Williams case. Williams died while in the custody of San Francisco police officers after officers subdued him and sprayed him with pepper spray in the Western Edition neighborhood in June 1995. Williams, a burglary suspect, was bound with wrist and ankle cuffs, and according to witnesses was hit and kicked after he was restrained. Departmental rules apparently were broken when the officers used pepper spray repeatedly on Williams, who appeared to be high on drugs, and officers did not monitor his breathing as required. One of the officers involved in the incident, Marc Andaya, had reportedly been the subject of as many as thirty-five complaints while working with the Oakland police force before being hired by the San Francisco Police Department. In Oakland, his supervisor reportedly had urged desk duty for Andaya because of his "cowboy" behavior. It is not clear why the San Francisco Police Department hired Andaya in light of his background, but the press reported that Andaya may have given only a partial account of his complaint history and no thorough check was conducted. Andaya was accused of neglect of duty and using excessive force, but the city's Police Commission initially deadlocked on the charges (two for, two against, with one police commissioner absent), which was in effect an exoneration. In large part due to community outrage over the Williams case, Andaya was eventually fired for lying about his disciplinary background in his application.

The Code of Silence

• A record of brutality complaints, inadequate supervision, and the code of silence were illustrated in the Anthony Baez case in New York City. Baez, age twenty-nine, was choked to death during an encounter with police Officer Francis X. Livoti on December 22, 1994. Livoti had been the subject of at least eleven brutality complaints over an eleven-year period, including one that was substantiated by the city's civilian review board involving the choking of a sixteen-year-old who was allegedly riding a go-cart recklessly. In the Baez case, Livoti was acquitted of criminally negligent homicide in a judge-only trial ending in October 1996. But in finding the prosecution's case unproven, the judge nevertheless criticized conflicting and inconsistent officer testimony, citing a "nest of perjury" within the department. Livoti was then prosecuted administratively to ascertain, in part, whether he had broken departmental rules that prohibit applying a choke hold. Partially in response to substantial publicity and community outrage over Livoti's behavior, he was fired in February 1997 for breaking departmental rules.

• The case of Frank Schmidt in Philadelphia illustrated flawed investigative procedures and lax discipline. Officer Christopher Rudy was on duty but reportedly visiting friends and drinking alcohol at a warehouse in November 1993. A dispute arose between the warehouse owner and Frank Schmidt, with Schmidt accused of stealing items from the warehouse. Schmidt reportedly told investigators that the warehouse gates were locked behind him, a gun was put to his head, and he was beaten as Officer Rudy watched and poured beer over Schmidt's head. Throughout the ordeal, the warehouse owner reportedly threatened to cut off Schmidt's hands with a knife and to have warehouse workers rape him. Schmidt reported the incident to the police, but Rudy was not questioned for seven months and then denied everything. Rudy reportedly received a twelve-day suspension for failing to take police action and for conduct unbecoming a police officer; he was returned to active duty.

Lax Oversight

• Lax oversight and the failure to act quickly to dismiss an abusive officer while he was still on probation were evident in Minneapolis. Officer Michael Ray Parent was convicted in state court of kidnaping and raping a woman in his squad car and was sentenced to four years in prison in April 1995. In the early morning hours of August 5, 1994, Officer Parent stopped and questioned the woman. She acknowledged she had been drinking, and he put her in the back seat of his squad car and told her she was under arrest for driving under the influence of alcohol. He then forced her to have oral sex with him. After the incident was reported, investigators found several prior complaints about Parent involving inappropriate sexual conduct while on duty, even though he had been on the force for only a year and a half before the August 1994 incident; he had been accused of a sexual incident during his probationary period on the force, when dismissals are much easier.

• Despite a civil jury trial leading to one of Indianapolis's largest awards following a judgment against an officer who fatally shot a burglary suspect, the officer remains on the force. Officer Wayne Sharp, who is white, shot and killed Edmund Powell, who was black, in June 1991. Sharp, a veteran officer, claimed the shooting was accidental and that Powell had swung a nail-studded board at him, yet according to at least one witness, Powell was on the ground and had apparently surrendered when he was shot. According to witnesses, Powell allegedly stole something from a department store, and Sharp chased him into an alley with his gun drawn. The Marion County prosecutor brought the case before a grand jury, and it declined to indict Sharp on any criminal charges. Community activists claimed that the shooting was racially motivated; Sharp had killed a black burglary suspect ten years earlier and a grand jury had declined to indict him. At that time, Sharp reportedly was removed from street duty because of his "flirtation" with the National Socialist White People's Party, a neo-Nazi group. Powell's grandmother, Gertrude Jackson, alleging Sharp intentionally shot Powell, filed a civil lawsuit in 1992; the jury found in favor of Jackson and awarded $465,000 to Powell's family. The city had not paid Jackson as of September 1997, and the status of any appeal was unclear. Despite his history, Sharp was still on duty as of mid-1997 and according to the police chief there has received "high accolades and several awards for superior work."

Enforcers Break the Rules

• A ranking New Orleans officer who himself was responsible for enforcing internal rules had a long history of abuse complaints, some sustained, but was only dismissed after he was convicted of a crime. Lieutenant Christopher Maurice was the subject of more than a dozen discourtesy and brutality complaints before being charged and convicted on two counts of simple battery in November 1995 (and fired two weeks later). The charges stemmed from a June 1994 incident in which Lt. Maurice allegedly slammed the head of radio personality Richard Blake (known as Robert Sandifer) against the police car's hood. Just after this encounter, Maurice was found in violation of department rules for getting into an argument and nearly a fistfight with a fellow officer during ethics training in early 1994. Also in June 1994, Maurice was served a warrant for another battery charge in St. Tammany Parish. Prior to the 1994 incidents, he had been suspended once (allegedly for brandishing his gun at a neighbor) and reprimanded twice since 1985, according to his civil service records. In a 1991 civil suit, the city paid a $25,000 settlement to a man who claimed that Maurice had hit him in the head with his police radio. Despite this record, Maurice was the commander in charge of enforcing the internal rules of the department. The city's citizen review agency (an external monitoring office) reportedly investigated several of the complaints against Maurice but did not uphold any of them as valid.

Police Must Be Scrutinized

Human Rights Watch recognizes that police officers, like other people, will make mistakes when they are under pressure to make split-second decisions regarding the use of force. Even the best recruiting, training, and command oversight will not result in flawless behavior on the part of all officers. Furthermore, we recognize that policing in the United States is a dangerous job. During 1996, 116 officers died while on duty nationwide (from all causes—shootings, assaults, accidents, and natural causes). Yet, precisely because police officers can make mistakes, or allow personal bias or emotion to enter into policing—and because they are allowed, as a last resort, to use potentially lethal force to subdue individuals they apprehend—police must be subjected to intense scrutiny.

The abuses described in this report are preventable. Officers with long records of abuse, policies that are overly vague, training that is substandard, and screening that is inadequate all create opportunities for abuse. Perhaps most important, and consistently lacking, is a system of oversight in which supervisors hold their charges accountable for mistreatment and are themselves reviewed and evaluated, in part, by how they deal with subordinate officers who commit human rights violations. Those who claim that each high-profile case of abuse by a "rogue" officer is an aberration are missing the point: problem officers frequently persist because the accountability systems are so seriously flawed.

Police, state, and federal authorities are responsible for holding police officers accountable for abusive or arbitrary acts. Police officials must ensure that police officers are punished when they violate administrative rules, while state and federal prosecutors must prosecute criminal acts committed by officers, and where appropriate, complicity by their superior officers. Each of these entities apply different standards when reviewing officer responsibility for an alleged abuse. All of these authorities have an obligation to ensure that the conduct of police officers meets international standards that prohibit human rights violations and that, in general, the U.S. complies with the obligations imposed by those treaties to which it is a party. While only the federal government is responsible for reporting internationally on U.S. compliance with the relevant treaties, local and state officials share responsibility for ensuring compliance within their jurisdictions.

> "*If anything, police departments pay more attention to the prevention of abuse in their recruitment and training policies than ever before.*"

The Extent of Police Brutality Is Exaggerated

Arch Puddington

In the following viewpoint, Arch Puddington maintains that while no statistics on police abuse in the United States are actually compiled, anecdotal evidence suggests that police brutality is waning and that police accountability is increasing. Puddington also argues that charges of police racism are unfair and asserts that minority police officers make up the majority of police departments in many major cities. Puddington is vice president for research at Freedom House, an organization that advances democratic values and opposes dictatorships worldwide.

As you read, consider the following questions:
1. According to Puddington, what was the purpose of Helsinki Watch?
2. What powerful reports has Human Rights Watch issued concerning human rights worldwide, according to the author?
3. What are "quality-of-life" crimes, according to the author?

In July 1998, Human Rights Watch issued a report claiming that police brutality is "one of the most serious, enduring, and divisive human rights violations in the United States." The report is startling in at least two respects. First, Human Rights Watch usually trains its sights on the world's most vicious governments, not the domestic social problems of the United States. Second, while the report echoes previous investigations by civil libertarians of police-abuse cases, it goes an important step further by urging the widespread application of international law as a weapon against what it deems an epidemic of police violence against the American people.

A careful reading of the report, titled "Shielded from Justice: Police Brutality and Accountability in the United States," suggests that the group got things backwards. America does not have a human-rights problem. Human Rights Watch, on the other hand, does seem to have an America problem: It neither understands nor appreciates the workings of democracy in its own backyard.

The History of Human Rights Watch

Human Rights Watch emerged out of Helsinki Watch, perhaps the most prominent of the private organizations established during the 1970s to monitor Soviet compliance with the 1975 Helsinki accords. Human Rights Watch began its work without ideological bias, and it earned a reputation as a sharp critic of the Soviet Union's failures to live up to its international obligations. It later became a fierce opponent of the Reagan administration's Central America policies, in particular its support of the government of El Salvador, then involved in a civil war against Marxist insurgents, and of the Nicaraguan contras, the anti-Communist group that was attempting to overthrow the leftist Sandinista regime.

Since the end of the Cold War, Human Rights Watch has actually expanded its mission. The organization maintains separate projects to monitor the observance of human rights in every part of the world, and continues to issue meticulously researched and often quite powerful reports on such diverse subjects as repression in Kashmir, atrocities in East Timor, and the inhumane treatment of handicapped children in China. At the same time, the group has ventured into several new areas: It has devoted more attention to the persecution of minority groups and launched ambitious projects to publicize violations of the rights of women and homosexuals. Recent reports have thus dealt with such issues as the enforced prostitution of young girls in Asia and discrimination against homosexuals in Romania.

A Shifting Focus

A further sign of the organization's shifting focus is the criticism it now directs at alleged patterns of human-rights violations in the United States. To be sure, from the beginning Human Rights Watch has been a vociferous critic of aspects of American foreign policy, a tradition it carries forward today through its pointed attacks on the Clinton administration for its refusal to sign various international treaties, most recently that concerning the International Criminal Court. The group also publishes regular reports on such issues as the treatment of women in U.S. prisons, the death penalty, and alleged misconduct of Border Patrol agents along the U.S.-Mexican border.

But the report on police abuse is the organization's most ambitious such investigation, and the most tendentious. As Human Rights Watch notes, police abuse is something over which Americans are deeply divided, especially along racial lines. But does police misconduct amount to a human-rights violation, a phrase that suggests crimes perpetrated by the state, sanctioned by the state, or tolerated by the state? The report conveys no doubts on this score. It carries a message of rampant police violence and official indifference. It contends that police brutality is "pervasive," that police racism is undiminished, and that abuse goes "unchecked" by higher authorities. Besides being exaggerated and sometimes downright wrong, these conclusions are contradicted by the facts in the report itself.

The Report Contradicts Itself

There is, to begin with, the question of whether police abuse has become more prevalent in recent years. Although the report's language often suggests that police brutality has reached epidemic proportions, the truth is that national statistics on police abuse are not compiled. The considerable anecdotal evidence in the report suggests that in some cities police abuse is declining. Nor does the report sustain the charge that police officials are passive towards misconduct in the ranks or, as was sometimes true in the past, actually encourage the worst instincts of law-enforcement officers. American cities no longer hire Frank Rizzos [Philadelphia mayor and police commissioner in the 1970s who had a reputation for aggressive policies] to run their police departments. Indeed, as the report indicates, police departments in a number of cities have implemented reform measures, such as improved training of recruits to reduce the chances of abusive behavior, and have stiffened disciplinary procedures to punish abusive officers.

The individual cases of alleged police brutality cited throughout the report—including the high-profile Rodney King episode in Los Angeles [in which King led police on a high-speed chase that ended in the televised police beating of King]—are apparently intended to demonstrate the barriers to justice in the current system. Here again, however, the careful reader might reach the opposite conclusion. In case after case, offending officers were in fact brought to justice, often even imprisoned. Sometimes, it's true, these cases extended over years and required several trials. But in this, police-abuse cases are not so different from other criminal cases where the accused make effective use of procedural protections to delay or evade punishment. What's more, as the American system has evolved through the years, an abusive police officer faces the prospect not merely of an investigation by his own department's internal affairs unit, but of state or federal criminal prosecution and punishment leading to years in prison. The victims of police abuse also have the option of seeking justice through civil lawsuits; as Human Rights Watch notes, millions of dollars have been paid to abuse victims in recent years.

Police Racism Is Exaggerated

Not surprisingly, the report gives special emphasis to the racial dimension of conflict between police and the public. "Race continues to play a central role in police brutality," the report alleges. "Indeed, despite gains in many areas since the civil rights movement of the 1950s and 1960s, one area that has been stubbornly resistant to change has been the treatment afforded minorities by police."

This is the kind of sweeping, superficial, and ultimately inaccurate assertion that one might expect from a domestic cause group, but not from a human-rights organization that prides itself on disentangling reality from conventional wisdom. For example, to buttress its claim of massive police racism, the report on more than one occasion notes that abuse claims by minority citizens are proportionately higher than their presence in the overall population. For purposes of comparison, however, the relevant statistic is not the minority presence in the local population, but the frequency with which minorities come in contact with the criminal-justice system. When this comparison is employed, the results suggest that complaints by black persons of police abuse are only slightly disproportionate or not disproportionate at all. Furthermore, there is the fact, not mentioned by Human Rights Watch, that minorities comprise a majority or near-majority of police officers in a number of the cities investigated for the report, and that black chiefs of police run the departments of an even larger number of big cities, including Los Angeles, Houston, Atlanta, Detroit, and New Orleans. Such developments do not ordinarily occur in systems that are "stubbornly resistant to change."

Improved Accountability

Where the report gives a distorted picture of police-minority relations, it skirts the role of police unions and civil-service rules in thwarting the expeditious and fair resolution of abuse cases. Most states have adopted laws intended to protect police officers and other civil servants from arbitrary or politically motivated reprisal. In practice, though, these measures also severely restrict the authority of a police chief to discipline abusive officers. Even in cases where department officials have dismissed officers for repeated acts of brutality, the officers have sometimes won reinstatement through legal appeals or the arbitration process. Yet while the report explains the impediments to effective discipline posed by certain civil-service procedures, it refrains from calling for major changes, an uncharacteristically cautious approach in a report that otherwise demands thorough-going change. . . .

Brutality Is Rare

While no one condones police brutality, many cops say that the context in which alleged brutality cases occur is often neither understood nor explained well by members of the media, who tend to demonize cops involved. "I'm out there sweating bullets, my heart's going 95 miles per hour and some guy is sitting in an air-conditioned office telling me what I should have done," said Dallas, Texas, police officer Jay James in 1990, referring to reporters. James had been the subject of an investigation after he shot at but missed a suspect who was waving a gun.

[Journalist Jon] Katz says it is surprising how rare cases of police violence against citizens are, given the demands placed on officers and the environment in which they work. Katz claims that in large cities such as New York City, the number of deaths attributed to officers has declined over the past two decades, despite the increase in illegal handguns and high-power weaponry that officers now need to defend themselves against.

In a study of the use of force by police in America's largest cities, William Geller and Michael Scott of the Police Executive Research Forum found that police shootings of civilians are relatively rare. Scott and Geller reported that a policeman in New York City would need to work for 694 years before the officer would be statistically expected to kill a criminal or other civilian. For officers in Milwaukee, Wisconsin, the figure is 1,299 years and in Chicago, the figure is 594 years.

Issues and Controversies On File, May 17, 1996.

The timing of the Human Rights Watch report suggests a . . . desire to dress up as an appeal to human rights—and to international law—what is in fact a condemnation of American policies with which the report's drafters find themselves in political disagreement. Although the United States has recently experienced a number of well-publicized police-brutality cases, the same could be said for any period since the 1960s. If anything, police departments pay more attention to the prevention of abuse in their recruitment and training policies than ever before.

At the same time, police departments in many cities have recently adopted more aggressive law-enforcement tactics, notably in cracking down on so-called quality-of-life crimes, such as public urination, the open use or sale of drugs, subway fare-beating, and similar non-violent offenses.

The emphasis on quality-of-life enforcement began in New York at the instigation of Mayor Rudolph Giuliani in 1994 and has been credited by many New Yorkers with making the city safer, more civil, and in general a better place to live. Although some minority spokesmen have complained that the new policy has led to an increase in police abuse, others have credited the new tougher line with having contributed to the revival of declining neighborhoods, including Harlem. Other cities have taken note of the steep decline in crime rates in New York, and have instituted similar policing tactics.

Human Rights Watch takes a dim view of quality-of-life policing, is disturbed by its popularity with the public, and objects to Giuliani's law-and-order policies. In this, it echoes the views of the New York Civil Liberties Union.

Going Global

The NYCLU's parent organization, the American Civil Liberties Union, has, of course, played a central role in the ongoing debate over American law enforcement for decades, and is best known for having spearheaded the legal effort to broaden the rights of criminal defendants. In recent years, the ACLU perspective has suffered a series of legislative setbacks, of which New York state's decision to reinstate the death penalty is the most vivid example. And where in the past the civil-liberties movement often won change in criminal-law procedures through the courts, in recent years the pendulum has swung in the opposite direction, as the federal judiciary has issued decisions that have restricted the rights of criminal defendants.

There is a considerable overlap of personnel between the ACLU and the lawyers and scholars who served as consultants to the Human Rights Watch report on police abuse. This is consistent with a pattern in which liberal and leftist cause organizations, having failed to win change through the normal channels of American democracy, "go global" to press their issues through international treaties and institutions, especially the U.N. With an American public strongly supportive of the kind of stepped-up crime-fighting techniques undertaken in New York, it is understandable that civil libertarians and groups like Human Rights Watch might turn in frustration to international law for a solution that they cannot now win domestically.

Democracy Is the Solution

They are, however, seriously mistaken in believing that reform can be promoted by "globalizing" the social problems of democracies. Indeed, the very suggestion betrays an astonishing lack of faith in the American democratic system and a misunderstanding of the process of winning political change in this country. More so than any other system, American democracy is flexible and open to adjustment. But Americans quite rightly resist change that is imposed by institutions not subject to popular control. They are certain to resist the notion that specialists in international law are better equipped to pass judgment on the system's shortcomings than Americans themselves.

"Shielded From Justice" never explains why the United States should recognize the authority of international law and global institutions. The report's authors presumably thought the answer to be self-evident. This in itself explains why Human Rights Watch, despite its impressive record in publicizing and protesting the crimes of the world's dictators, is not likely to exert a similar influence in the debate over social reform in the United States.

| "Cops must . . . stop using the 'few bad apples' defense to obscure the fact that the code of silence among honest cops is allowing crooked and racist cops to flourish."

Police Corruption Is Widespread

Joseph D. McNamara

Joseph D. McNamara argues in the following viewpoint that the number of police corruption cases nationwide is rising due to public pressure to reduce crime. He asserts that police departments have developed an "anything goes" attitude as they strive to apprehend suspects and establish winnable cases against them. Recent corruption cases have led to greater self-scrutiny by police departments, McNamara contends, but, he warns, public trust will not be restored until police departments stop tolerating and covering up corruption. McNamara, a research fellow at the Hoover Institution at Stanford University, is the retired police chief of San Jose.

As you read, consider the following questions:

1. According to McNamara, what crime is a New Orleans cop accused of?
2. What kind of corruption did the FBI uncover in its own ranks?
3. What does the author claim is the essential task of police agencies in their fight against police corruption?

Reprinted from "America's Plague of Bad Cops," by Joseph D. McNamara, *Los Angeles Times*, September 17, 1995, p. M-2, by permission of the author.

Citizens are having trouble distinguishing the good guys from the bad. Retired LAPD [Los Angeles Police Department] Detective Mark Fuhrman spouts venomous racism and brags to an aspiring screenwriter about torturing, beating and framing suspects. Cops across the country murder people, pull armed robberies while in uniform, sell dope, steal drug-buy money, shake down criminals, accept bribes and falsify evidence against criminal defendants. The standard defense coming from law enforcement is that only a relative handful of the 400,000 cops nationwide go bad. For several reasons, the public is not reassured.

More Bad Cops

First, the number of reported cases of bad cops is rising. Some L.A. County deputy sheriffs get caught robbing and extorting money from drug dealers. In New Orleans, a uniformed cop is accused of murdering her partner and shop owners during a robbery committed while she was on patrol. In Washington, D.C., and in Atlanta, cops in drug stings are arrested for stealing and taking bribes. In Boston, two white cops frame a black man for murdering a white woman. New York State troopers falsify evidence that sends people to prison. In San Francisco, counterfeit evidence means hundreds of drug convictions are likely to be overturned. Similar evidence tampering forces the prosecution to reopen many cases in Philadelphia.

It's not just the rank and file, either. The former police chief of Detroit is in prison for stealing drug-buy money. In a small New England town, the chief steals drugs from the evidence locker for his own use. A number of Southern sheriffs are convicted of being in league with drug smugglers.

Agencies thought to be untouchable are suddenly reaping as many bad headlines as the perennially troubled New York City Police Department. The Drug Enforcement agent who arrested Panama's Gen. Manuel Noriega on drug-trafficking charges is in jail for stealing laundered drug money. The FBI catches one of its agents taking drugs from the evidence stockpile and trying to market them to regional drug dealers.

Of course, police corruption is not new. The heritage of cops in America includes corruption, racism and abuse of power for political purposes. The urban police forces started in the 1840s followed the orders of political machines like Tammany Hall [site of New York City's Democratic Party which was then known for corruption]. Aficionados of Raymond Chandler's private eye, Philip Marlowe, will recall his good luck in encountering an occasional honest cop as he roamed Southern California in the 1930s. Ironically, it was the LAPD—whose recent problems have amplified police departments' sins nationwide—under the leadership of William H. Parker, that first gained its freedom from politics to become a professional force.

Reprinted by permission of David Sipress.

One of the fundamental problems of American policing is the conflict between law-enforcement duties and maintaining order in the streets. For example, the Los Angeles Police Department is probably the most arrest-happy department in the country. By contrast, cops in other cities send drunks home, overlook minor violations and seek to keep the streets calm without resorting to arrest. Also, the LAPD, as well as other police forces, maintain control by aggressively policing minority communities. Resisters are taught a lesson and, if necessary, punished physically, especially if they show "contempt of cop." Politicians and officials whose careers depend on tough-on-crime rhetoric are reluctant to ask too many questions about what the cops are doing.

Indeed, public fear of crime has made it increasingly difficult for the relatively small number of police chiefs who really care to get civil-service commissions to uphold discipline in their ranks. And the few district attorneys willing to prosecute cops for unnecessary use of force find it difficult to get juries to convict officers, especially when the victim of a police beating is a minority. After all, in a "war," you cannot tie your soldiers' hands when the "enemy" is so dangerous.

Police Must Police Themselves

True, American policing has greatly improved since the civil rights movement directed attention to police abuses. But the recent outbreak of bad-cop problems has cost police forces a lot of the credibility they had gained among minority groups with good policing. Still, there is one silver lining in the cloud of distrust created by the Fuhrman tapes and the plethora of police scandals: more self-scrutiny.

We should not, however, make the mistake of getting lost in debates about such reform mechanisms as civilian-review boards, community policing and special prosecutors. Rather, the essential task is to create within police agencies an incentive to break the code of silence among the rank and file and encourage cops to police themselves. A corrupt, racist or brutal cop will abstain from misconduct only when he looks at the cop next to him and believes that the officer will blow the whistle if he hits the suspect. The police value system is what permits the kind of behavior that gets bad headlines. Real reform is possible only when that value system changes and cops come to realize that they must police themselves.

For mayors and chiefs, the first step is to stop telling cops they are engaged in war. Next, they and rank-and-file cops must also stop using the "few bad apples" defense to obscure the fact that the code of silence among honest cops is allowing crooked and racist cops to flourish. Finally, leaders should be honest and acknowledge that good cops are now punished, instead of rewarded, if they expose bad cops. Politicians and chiefs must recognize that it is not negative publicity to weed out misfits; it actually demonstrates to the public that it can trust the police to police themselves.

Only when the community can tell the good guys from the bad will we be able to get tough on crime. Then, people will report crime to the police, serve as witnesses and, when they sit on a jury, believe police testimony. Justice is not served when juries spend as much time judging the police as determining the guilt or innocence of the person on trial.

"Journalists are quick to look at the actions of a few and paint all officers as corrupt and power-hungry brutes."

The Extent of Police Corruption Is Exaggerated

Sunil Dutta

In the following viewpoint, Sunil Dutta argues that the media overgeneralize when they use one corrupt police officer to illustrate department-wide abuse. When departments discover corrupt officers, he contends, they should be disciplined swiftly. Dutta also asserts that police need to be held to higher moral standards than the general population. Dutta is a police officer in the Los Angeles Police Department's West Valley Division.

As you read, consider the following questions:
1. What is the author's background?
2. Why did the author join the Los Angeles Police Department?
3. What elements of police work affect the humanity of officers, according to Dutta?

Reprinted from "Cops Aren't Cloned in a Brutish Mold," by Sunil Dutta, *Los Angeles Times*, October 27, 1999, p. B-9, by permission of the author.

The past few weeks [of October 1999] have not been good for the Los Angeles Police Department [LAPD]. But just how pervasive are corruption and misconduct among police officers? Is this behavior systemic, or are the things described by Rafael A. Perez, the officer who blew the whistle on the Rampart Division, isolated cases? [Many officers within the Rampart Division of the LAPD were accused by Officer Perez of corruption including perjury, planting evidence and stealing drugs.]

Unfair Generalizations

While I do not condone the actions by Perez and other officers in Rampart or elsewhere, I believe that painting all the officers with the same brush based on actions of one or even several officers is grossly unfair.

I have three degrees in biology and have taught at the university level. I am the founder and president of a nonprofit organization promoting the 2,000-year-old ancient Indian classical music, Dhrupad. I am a published author of a poetry book and scientific manuscripts. Yet somehow I doubt that any reporter would take my background and depict all LAPD officers as scientists and authors.

However, journalists are quick to look at the actions of a few and paint all officers as corrupt and power-hungry brutes. This is no different from racist attitudes that say that if one Latino teenager is a gangster, all Latino teenagers must be gangsters, or that if one African American man commits a crime, all African American men are criminals.

Police Reflect Society

I joined the LAPD in part to observe police culture and study human nature. Several of my assumptions about police have changed as a result of working as an officer. I now recognize that some problems exist within police departments due to the nature of police work itself; interacting daily with hardened criminals, victims of violence and abusive and manipulative people cannot help but affect the humanity of officers.

However, police departments do not exist in a vacuum. Officers represent the society they are part of, including all the problems that exist around them. Only a change in society and in societal expectations can bring change in institutions like a police department. Even a quick historical study of the LAPD or any other police department in America would show how the nature of policing continues to evolve in a positive direction.

Most Officers Are Honest

The vast majority of police officers throughout [New York City] do not engage in corruption. They are honest, hardworking men and women who perform difficult and dangerous duties each day with efficiency and integrity, doing their best to protect the people of our City. The horror many officers expressed at the 1993 revelations [that corruption exists in the New York City Police Department] was heartfelt and sincere.

Commission to Investigate Allegations of Police Corruption and the Anti-Corruption Procedures of the New York City Police Department Report, 1993.

In my two years at the LAPD, I have been impressed by the diversity, dedication and integrity of the people I work with. Many times I have seen officers exercise great restraint against aggressive and combative people when they justifiably could have used force. Of course we are faced with difficult decisions. But if my partner were to do something unethical, I would stop him, and I hope he would do the same for me.

I have so far not seen any officer misconduct in my division, which leads me to believe that systemic misconduct does not exist in the LAPD.

Officers Must Have Higher Standards

Police officers have powers that, if abused, can result in serious harm to people's lives and liberty. Officers must set a higher moral and ethical standard in their public and personal lives. Any misconduct charge must be seriously investigated and severe punishments meted out to the individuals who bring shame and dishonor to the badge. Rightfully, in the case of Rampart, the LAPD has shown itself capable of conducting a thorough investigation of alleged misconduct. We should remember that it was the LAPD's own investigation that eventually resulted in the misconduct charges coming to light.

Yes, we may have bad cops—and if we do, we need to eliminate them from the force. However, most of the officers I've come in contact with are honest and dedicated professionals. Their hard work should be acknowledged.

"The greatest danger to our lives and liberties comes primarily from arrogant, irresponsible, unaccountable law enforcement agencies such as the FBI."

The FBI Is Brutal and Corrupt

Phyllis Schlafly

In 1993, federal agents surrounded a compound in Waco, Texas, home of the Branch Davidians cult which was under investigation for amassing illegal weapons. The cult members refused to comply with a search warrant and a standoff between the Davidians and the FBI ensued. After fifty-one days, the FBI inserted tear gas into the buildings, and shortly thereafter the compound caught fire, resulting in the deaths of eighty-six cult members and four federal agents. In the following viewpoint, Phyllis Schlafly argues that during the Waco siege, the FBI killed innocent civilians who posed no threat to the community. She maintains that federal law enforcement agencies such as the FBI pose a grave danger to the public because they cannot be trusted to act responsibly and hold themselves accountable for their actions. Phyllis Schlafly is founder of the Eagle Forum, a conservative pro-family organization.

As you read, consider the following questions:
1. According to Schlafly, how many children died in the Waco fires?
2. Why did the Clinton administration support the FBI's actions against the Branch Davidians, in the author's view?
3. In the author's opinion, why did the Branch Davidians shoot the ATF agents?

Reprinted from "The Waco Scandal Just Won't Go Away," by Phyllis Schlafly, *Eagle Forum*, September 8, 1999, by permission of the author.

J anet Reno [U.S. attorney general under the Clinton administration] is shocked, shocked to discover that the FBI has been lying for six years about the 1993 Waco debacle.

The Waco fire burned up 86 members of a religious cult called Branch Davidians (including 24 children, 17 of whom were younger than age 10), and has kept eight survivors rotting in prison ever since, serving long sentences denounced by the jury that heard the evidence. But it was a career-enhancer for Janet Reno, who at that time was President Clinton's most controversial Cabinet appointment, widely criticized by both right and left.

Cover-Ups

Immediately after the Waco fire, she starred in an Academy Award–worthy performance before a Congressional committee, defending the FBI's actions to the hilt, confidently taking personal responsibility for all of the government's actions, and asserting that she would make the same decisions if she had the chance to do it all over again. Suddenly, the same people who were criticizing her began to praise her.

Now, after six years of categorical denials that the FBI fired potentially flammable tear gas canisters at the Branch Davidians on their final day, Janet Reno has ordered the FBI to investigate itself. That's like asking the Clinton White House staff to investigate Bill Clinton's lies about Monica Lewinski [a White House aide with whom Clinton was alleged to have had sexual relations].

Will the FBI investigate whether Janet Reno was lying for six years or was negligent and incompetent in not extracting the truth from the FBI before she went public to defend all their actions? Contrary to her 1993 assertions, she did not take responsibility for Waco; she only said she did, thereby facilitating the cover-up.

The Religious Cult Was Not a Threat

Why did the Clinton Administration attack a small and pitiful religious cult with a full-scale military offensive, using 700 men, machine guns, army tanks, and the secret, highly trained U.S. Delta military force created for use against dangerous terrorists? Why did the FBI spend six hours pouring into the compound the gas known as CS, which is banned for use in war by the Chemical Weapons Treaty?

This came after a 51-day siege of their compound, during which the government cut off the Davidians' water and electricity, and tormented them with recordings of animal screams played at a deafening high pitch.

Flagrant Abuse of Power

Waco is about a flagrant abuse of government power, including the use of military weapons, tanks and helicopters to attack U.S. citizens. It is about anti-gun zealotry, religious bigotry, fraudulent drug charges and a callous attitude toward the safety of pregnant women, innocent babies and small children.

Linda Bowles, *New York Times*, July 30, 1995.

All the excuses that Janet Reno proffered in her original defense of the FBI have been proven to be false. The cult wasn't any threat to others, it wasn't peddling illegal drugs, it wasn't engaged in unlawful child abuse, and its members had fewer guns per person than the average gun ownership of Texans.

Murder and Revenge

Did the Clinton Administration simply decide to murder the Branch Davidians to avenge the deaths of the four BATF (Bureau of Alcohol, Tobacco and Firearms) agents a few weeks before the fatal final day? There is said to be a tradition among federal law enforcement personnel that, if one of their agents is killed, his buddies go after the killers and gun them down in speedy capital retribution, without waiting for such niceties as a trial, due process, or conviction.

Of course, that isn't written in any law or rules of procedure; it just happens. Some will justify that behavior as appropriate retaliation after an agent is gunned down in cold blood, but that wasn't what happened at Waco. The Branch Davidians were arguably acting in self-defense against the surprise invasion of their home by BATF agents who fired wildly and killed ten cult members.

On the day of the final assault, the FBI kept newsmen and

television cameras on the side of the building where they couldn't see the real military offensive. Fortunately a plane overhead took pictures that millions of Americans have seen in the film, *Waco: Rules of Engagement.*

The FBI lies have become front-page news [in September 1999] because of a statement by the civilian overseer of the Texas Rangers. However, the plaintiffs in the wrongful death civil suits brought by the relatives of the Branch Davidians still haven't been allowed to do the kind of discovery that federal rules allow, so much more is still hidden by the FBI-Reno cover-up.

Federal Agents Are Dangerous

As in other scandals of recent years, the government's cover-up has compounded its original errors. The Democrats closed ranks to protect Clinton's appointees in the Justice Department and the FBI, and the Republicans dropped the ball because of their traditional mindset in favor of law enforcement.

The danger America faces today is not from tiny, misguided religious cults. The greater danger to our lives and liberties comes primarily from arrogant, irresponsible, unaccountable law enforcement agencies such as the FBI and the BATF, especially when using the military for domestic law enforcement.

The FBI lied to the American people and clearly wasn't to be trusted about Waco.

"Critics currently attacking the FBI are putting at risk one of the most valuable assets this country has."

Charges Against the FBI Are Exaggerated

Oliver "Buck" Revell

Over eighty members of the Branch Davidian cult and four federal agents were killed at the conclusion of a fifty-one day siege in Waco, Texas, in 1993. In the following viewpoint, Oliver "Buck" Revell argues that although the FBI and other federal agencies involved in the Waco siege committed many mistakes, they did not murder anyone or attempt to cover up or lie about their actions during the siege. In fact, Revell maintains, the FBI continues to support thorough investigations into its conduct and deserves a fair and impartial evaluation. Revell, now chairman of the Greater Dallas Crime Commission, was the associate deputy director of the FBI and provided support to the FBI's operation during the Waco siege.

As you read, consider the following questions:
1. According to Revell, how did the FBI establish that David Koresh had no intention of surrendering?
2. Why did the FBI decide to insert CS gas into the compound, according to the author?
3. According to the author, who conducted the investigation that determined that the Davidians had set the fires?

Reprinted from "Stop Looking for Scapegoats," by Oliver "Buck" Revell, *San Diego Union-Tribune*, p. G-1, October 10, 1999, by permission of the author.

In February 1993, a calamitous situation developed when agents for the Bureau of Alcohol, Tobacco and Firearms [ATF] descended upon the Branch Davidian compound just outside Waco, Texas. They went to arrest Davidian leader David Koresh for weapons violations at a place called Mt. Carmel. The tragedy that followed continues to haunt the ATF, the FBI and the Justice Department.

Cult Was Collecting Firearms and Grenades

In the months before the raid, local and state agencies, as well as the ATF, had developed information indicating that the Davidians were illegally collecting huge quantities of firearms, grenades, ammunition and bomb-making materials. So on Feb. 28 the ATF executed a woefully ill-conceived raid.

Some local media were alerted, and they in turn alerted the Davidians. After a 45-minute exchange of gunfire, four ATF agents were dead and 15 injured. The number of casualties of the Davidians was not known at the time, but the FBI knew several were killed and wounded. The ATF then pulled back, and a long standoff ensued.

Later that day, President Bill Clinton ordered the FBI to take over. Jeff Jamar of the San Antonio field office was in charge of what was a difficult situation from the beginning. There was no advantage of surprise by the FBI. The best its officials could hope for was that the hostage negotiators would coax the 33-year-old religious fanatic and his heavily armed followers out of the building.

Cult Leader Would Not Surrender

Koresh had no intention of surrendering. His intention to thwart any attempt to surrender by his followers was clearly established by electronic surveillance devices (all court-approved) that the FBI smuggled into the compound. The intelligence also revealed the discussion of a "suicide by cop" break-out strategy whereby Koresh and his "mighty men," Koresh's palace guard, would storm out of the compound, killing as many FBI agents as they could before being killed, captured or escaping.

The new attorney general, Janet Reno, was especially worried that the human waste and corpses of those killed in the

ATF raid could spread disease. This concern gradually led to the consensus that the standoff could not continue indefinitely.

Jamar crafted a plan for using M-60 tanks to insert CS gas into the compound. This kind of tear gas was more effective than CN tear gas because it was non-flammable and did not pose a threat to the women and children in the compound. The purpose of using the tear gas was to drive the cultists out of the compound. Everyone on site realized the Davidians might decide to commit mass suicide like Jim Jones and his cultist followers had 15 years earlier, but most experts the FBI consulted did not think this was likely.

Reno and President Clinton approved the plan to use the tanks to insert the gas, and on the morning of April 19, the FBI moved in while over the loudspeaker the Davidians were instructed not to fire. An hour later the tanks began punching holes in the walls and filling the building with a mist of gas. The Davidians immediately opened fire, though the agents would not fire a single shot in return.

A Gigantic Fireball Filled the Sky

A couple of hours into the operation, a tank began knocking down the doors so the Davidians could get out. Shortly after noon, fires within the compound could be seen. Eventually, a gigantic fireball and a plume of black smoke leapt into the sky. Gunfire cracked from within the compound. The Davidians were killing themselves, and FBI agents could do little more than watch helplessly.

During congressional hearings, Reno explained the FBI's actions and the reasoning behind each. She also took responsibility for the tragic outcome. The FBI should have given her better advice. There should have been a better plan. The FBI should have been prepared for a fire.

Yet accusations that the FBI had deliberately set the fire and intentionally caused the deaths of the Davidians are blatant and intentional lies. The FBI did not cause the fires or kill anyone. Its officials desperately wanted to get all Davidians out of the compound safely. Koresh and his lieutenants were responsible for the deaths at Mt. Carmel, and no one else.

By agreement between the Justice Department and the Texas Department of Public Safety, the Texas Rangers conducted an independent investigation at the compound, and no one who had participated in the standoff or gas insertion was allowed to collect evidence from the burned compound. The Rangers brought in fire marshals and arson experts. The independent team determined that the Davidians had set the fires.

Reno, meanwhile, appointed Ed Dennis, a Republican and former assistant attorney general of the criminal division and U.S. attorney in Philadelphia, as the special counsel to conduct an inquiry. Dennis recommended improvements in the decision-making process, but he did not fault the decision to use tear gas. He also established that the FBI had made a good-faith effort to obtain the safe release of all minors and women and the peaceful surrender of the men.

The Waco Siege Was Court Approved

The people whom I've seen quoted in saying that [Waco] was some government plot, some kind of harsh, totalitarian attack on a group of innocent people, carried out in a ruthless, lawless manner—that's just not what happened. It isn't true and people should know that. It was a law-enforcement action [undertaken with] court-approved search and arrest warrants.

Edwin O. Guthman, *Los Angeles Times*, April 26, 1995.

Recent revelations about the Waco episode based upon ongoing civil litigation and research by the producers of a so-called documentary have raised troubling questions about the use of military tear gas at the scene. (The tear gas was pyrotechnic, not incendiary, as some in the media have described it.)

We know that Reno thought she had prohibited the use of such devices. We know that both Bob Ricks, second in command at Waco, and Dan Coulson, a senior official at FBI headquarters, did not know pyrotechnic tear-gas devices had been used and did not authorize their use.

We also know that the hostage rescue team did use the devices and that Richard Rodgers, commander of the team, authorized their use. What we do not know, and this is a major point of contention, is why Rodgers thought he was authorized to use the devices.

Even so, the charges of a cover-up are unfounded. Why?

Because agents acknowledged the use of the devices in debriefings, and the results of these debriefings were shared with Justice Department attorneys, plaintiffs' attorneys in civil litigation and the congressional committees overseeing the Waco probe. This is hardly the way to conduct a "cover-up."

And Texas Rangers have managed the crime-scene investigation. This, too, hardly lends credence to the allegation of a cover-up by the FBI or the Justice Department.

Neither FBI Director Louis Freeh nor Reno has any reason to obstruct justice or commit perjury. I know both of them to be totally honest and dedicated public servants.

Critics currently attacking the FBI are putting at risk one of the most valuable assets this country has. It was bad enough when anti-government zealots loudly proclaimed that the government had deliberately sought to kill the Davidians, but now even thoughtful and moderate politicians and journalists are jumping on the bandwagon. Demands that either the FBI director or the attorney general resign over this controversial issue are ill-timed and certainly unwarranted.

No evidence shows a cover-up, obstruction of justice or perjury. Certainly, there are serious discrepancies in information about the Waco siege revealed six years ago and details released in recent weeks, and those discrepancies must be investigated and resolved. Newly appointed special counsel John Danforth, the widely respected former Republican senator from Missouri, will do just that.

Congress also should hold more Waco-related hearings after Danforth's investigation is complete. And the civil wrongful-death litigation under the jurisdiction of federal Judge Walter Smith of Waco should continue. After each of these independent fact-finding procedures is completed, officials can fix blame and punish specific wrongdoing—if any occurred.

The 25,000 men and women of the FBI who serve their country with dedication and often valor desire their day in court as well. They should not be found guilty of crimes or gross misconduct without due process. The American public needs an effective FBI, and today the entire organization is under attack by those who should know better.

Periodical Bibliography

The following articles have been selected to supplement the diverse views presented in this chapter. Addresses are provided for periodicals not indexed in the *Readers' Guide to Periodical Literature*, the *Alternative Press Index*, the *Social Sciences Index*, or the *Index to Legal Periodicals and Books*.

Peter Boyer	"Burned," *New Yorker*, November 1, 1999.
John Cloud	"L.A. Confidential, for Real," *Time*, September 27, 1999.
Commonweal	"Racial Politics," May 21, 1999.
Bob Herbert	"Beyond the Diallo Case," *New York Times*, April 4, 1999.
William F. Jasper	"Local Police Under Siege," *New American*, May 11, 1998. Available from 770 Westhill Blvd., Appleton, WI 54914.
Daniel Klaidman and Michael Isikoff	"Facing More Fire at the FBI," *Newsweek*, October 18, 1999.
Edward T. Lewis	"We Should Not Be Afraid," *Essence*, November 1999.
John McCormick	"On a High-Tech Firing Line," *Newsweek*, December 6, 1999.
Salim Muwakkil	"No Cop Accountability," *In These Times*, April 11, 1999.
Scott Pendleton	"Return to Waco: A Hard Search for Answers Amid the Ashes," *Christian Science Monitor*, July 18, 1995.
Arch Puddington	"The War on the War on Crime," *Commentary*, May 1999.
Carl Thomas Rowan	"D.C. Confidential," *New Republic*, January 19, 1998.
Henry Ruth	"The FBI Investigates Itself—Again," *Wall Street Journal*, August 30, 1999.
Mike Tharp	"The FBI's Sniper Under Fire," *U.S. News & World Report*, November 8, 1999.

What Factors Cause Police Brutality?

Chapter Preface

Henry Cornelius Brown Jr., brandishing two handguns, kneeled down outside a police station in Shelby, South Carolina, in 1997 and begged police to shoot him. Feeling that Brown posed a threat to their lives, the officers opened fire, killing him. Brown thus became another casualty in the phenomenon known as "suicide by cop."

Experts believe that 10 percent of the roughly six hundred fatal shootings a year by law enforcement are the result of people provoking police in a desire to end their own lives. Often, these shootings prompt charges of police brutality by the community. Those who incite police to kill them are mostly men in their twenties with drug or alcohol problems. As Alan Feuer, reporter for the *New York Times*, reports, most people who want police to kill them tend to "suffer from depression and are haunted by feelings of dependence and hopelessness." People who commit suicide by cop know that the police are trained to fire their weapons when they feel that their lives are in danger. Clinton Van Zandt of the FBI claims that provoking the police to kill is probably a surer way to die than taking tranquilizers.

One reason for the fatal shootings, experts say, is that the police are not trained adequately to defuse potentially dangerous encounters with people with mental illness. Mental health experts want police trained to recognize when a suspect is mentally ill and to handle confrontations by backing off and talking with the suspect.

A police officer's overarching goal is to save lives, not take them. Many police departments believe that with better training, more mentally disturbed suspects like Henry Cornelius Brown Jr. could be helped, not killed, and more police officers would be spared the emotional anguish of participating in someone else's suicide. Police departments also assert that learning to handle encounters with mentally distressed suspects will reduce charges of police brutality that often follow fatal shootings by police. A lack of training in how to handle the mentally ill is one of the issues debated by the authors in the following chapter.

"The list of [blacks killed by police officers with near impunity] is still not long enough to convince political leaders to effectively confront the racism responsible for these crimes."

Racism Causes Police Brutality

Salim Muwakkil

In the following viewpoint, Salim Muwakkil argues that in case after case, society allows white police officers to kill black suspects with impunity. Racism is endemic to American culture, Muwakkil maintains, and reflects the public's growing fear of black criminals. Muwakkil asserts that tough-on-crime policies and the criminal justice system are inadequate to solve problems that are deeply rooted in the racial history of the United States. Muwakkil is a senior editor at *In These Times*, a liberal biweekly publication.

As you read, consider the following questions:
1. According to Muwakkil, what was the purpose of the first U.S. organized police forces?
2. According to the Amnesty International report, how many police brutality charges were filed in 1994?
3. What was Peter Del Debbio's sentence for shooting a black officer, according to the author?

Reprinted from "Getting Away with Murder," by Salim Muwakkil, *In These Times*, January 6, 1997, by permission of *In These Times*.

On October 24 [1997], Officer James Knight shot and killed 18-year-old Tyrone Lewis, an unarmed black man, during a routine traffic stop in St. Petersburg, Florida. Lewis apparently failed to respond when Knight and his partner ordered him out of the car after pulling him over for speeding in the city's predominantly black south side. When Knight's partner broke one of the car windows, the car lurched forward, bumping Officer Knight, who then threatened to shoot. Lewis' car then reportedly lurched forward again, this time striking Knight forcefully. Knight fired his gun three times, shooting Lewis twice in the arm and once in the chest. Police later learned the car was stolen and that Lewis was wanted on three arrest warrants. But community residents who witnessed the incident insist that the police were never threatened.

An Antagonistic Relationship

Lewis' death sparked a riot in the resort city's African-American neighborhood. The disturbance covered a 20-square-block area; 29 buildings and many cars were set on fire. Eleven people were injured. The grand jury decision not to indict the police officer provoked another round of civil unrest three weeks later.

While so far only the black community in St. Petersburg has responded with such destructive rage, black neighborhoods across the country are seething with anger at the impunity enjoyed by police officers who kill black men.

Relations between African-Americans and the police have been antagonistic throughout U.S. history. The first organized police forces in this country were slave patrols created to keep enslaved Africans in check. The troubled relationship between blacks and the police has erupted sporadically in violence: Most of the "long hot summer" riots during the '60s were sparked by charges of police brutality. The urban unrest in Miami during the '80s was associated with allegations of police violence. And the nation's largest urban explosion occurred in Los Angeles following the 1992 acquittal of the police who brutalized motorist Rodney King.

The police are using deadly force more and more frequently these days—and getting away with it. The stories are eerily similar:

• July 30, 1995: Joseph Gould, an unarmed homeless black man, is shot to death outside a downtown Chicago nightclub by Gregory Becker, an off-duty white cop. The officer is initially charged with official misconduct, but vigorous protests convince the Illinois state attorney to increase the charge to armed violence. The city now anxiously awaits Becker's February trial [Becker was sentenced to fifteen years in prison in May 1997].

• October 3, 1995: Jorge Guillen, a Honduran immigrant, dies of suffocation in police custody in Chicago. The state attorney's office declines to prosecute the officers, citing lack of evidence of any criminal conduct. The Office of Professional Standards (OPS), an independent agency of civilian staffers considered by many to be in the pocket of the police, nevertheless concludes that the three officers involved used excessive force. The agency recommends that they receive short suspensions. The recommendation, however, is overruled on December 11, 1996, by the Chicago Police Board, which cites conflicting medical evidence and inconsistent witness statements.

• June 13, 1996: Aswan Keshawn Watson, an unarmed 21-year-old black man, is killed when three plainclothes officers fire 24 bullets into him during a drug raid in Brooklyn's Flatbush section.

• October 17, 1996: Aaron White, the black owner of a television repair shop in the west-central Mississippi town of Leland, is shot to death by a white policeman. Initially, police say the 29-year-old White was trying to escape from the scene of a traffic accident and fired first on Officer Jackie Blaylock, who successfully returned fire. The police later revise their story, saying White accidentally killed himself in the escape attempt.

• November 19, 1996: James Cooper, a black 19-year-old, is shot to death by Officer Michael Marlow during a traffic stop in Charlotte, North Carolina. The white officer tells investigators he fired because he thought Cooper was reaching for a gun. No gun is found, but Marlow is not charged.

Examples of blacks and other minorities killed by police officers with near impunity could fill three times this space. Unfortunately, the list is still not long enough to convince political leaders to effectively confront the racism responsible for these crimes.

Escalating police violence reflects a growing fear of black criminality among the broader population. The skyrocketing rate of black imprisonment and the profits to be made from the prison industry suggest that the criminal justice system and young African-Americans are increasingly becoming each other's sworn enemies.

Reprinted by permission of Kirk Anderson.

"Racist assumptions are built into the very foundation of American policing," says William Geller, associate director of the Police Executive Research Forum, a Washington-based group that studies law enforcement issues. Geller, the author of several books on police abuse, is not surprised by the ratcheting up of tensions between police and black men. The widening gap between the rich and the poor combined with the absence of well-paying jobs in urban America have placed these two populations at loggerheads, he says.

Amnesty International released a report in late June 1996 that documented a disturbing pattern of police violence in America's largest police force. Entitled "Police Brutality and Excessive Force in the New York City Police Department," the 72-page report found that the New York Police Department routinely violates international human rights standards as well as its own guidelines governing the use of deadly force. The 18-month investigation found that charges of police brutality in New York climbed from 977 in 1987 to more than 2,000 in 1994. Deaths in police custody rose from 11 in 1991 to 24 in 1994. According to the report, most of the victims were minorities, while most of the offending police officers were white. Amnesty International concluded that excessive use of force has probably led to many more deaths in police custody than the New York Police Department is willing to acknowledge. The report cited several cases in which men in custody subjected to choke holds or sprayed with capsicum pepper died of apparently related seizures or asphyxiation.

White Cops Shoot Black Cops

The report also noted a troubling new development: black undercover police officers being shot by their white colleagues. New York City transit officers Derwin Pannell and Desmond Robinson both were mistaken for criminals and shot by white officers. On November 18, 1992, Pannell was attempting to arrest a farebeater in a dark subway station in the Canarsie section of Brooklyn, when he was confronted by white transit officers who mistook him for a mugger because he was rifling through the woman's handbag with his gun drawn. In later testimony, Pannell said his fellow officers did not identify themselves before opening fire. A Brooklyn grand jury cleared Pannell's assailants of all charges.

Officer Robinson had his gun drawn and was in pursuit of a suspect on August 24, 1994, when he was mistaken for a criminal and shot by Peter Del Debbio, an off-duty police officer on his way home. Testimony and evidence in the case suggest that Del Debbio stood over Robinson as he lay helpless on the subway platform and shot him three times in the back. Del Debbio was convicted in March 1996 of second-degree assault and sentenced to 200 hours of community service and five years' probation.

New York City, of course, is not the only place where white cops have mistakenly shot black cops. In Nashville,

Reggie Miller, a black cop, was working on an undercover prostitution sting when five white police officers pulled him over for a traffic violation and forced him to the ground. The officers didn't give Miller the opportunity to identify himself, and within minutes they began beating him for no apparent reason. The offending officers were initially dismissed from the police force, but were later reinstated by the city's civil service commission.

Deep Social Wounds

The Amnesty International report may cause a temporary spasm of civic embarrassment in New York, but if previous experience in Chicago and Los Angeles is any indication, don't expect much to change. Amnesty International issued a 1990 report describing police torture and brutality in Chicago and an equally scathing 1992 report on the Los Angeles Police Department. Neither the police nor their political overseers in either city have moved to address the concerns raised in those reports.

Rampant Racism

Open racism and hidden white supremacist involvement are a serious problem among [many] police forces. In Houston, where the [Ku Klux] Klan has been waging an active recruitment campaign among the police for over a year [in 1998], a police corporal, Al Csaszar, was put on paid leave in July 1998 after beating a Nigerian immigrant and yelling racist epithets at him. In June, Boynton Beach, Florida, police officer Dave Demarest sought reinstatement to the department after having been fired in February for having flaunted a swastika tattoo to several other cops, including a Jewish woman officer.

Turning the Tide, Winter/Spring 1998.

"All of this is part of a larger crackdown on African-Americans," says political scientist and author Andrew Hacker. "White Americans have decided that enough is enough. They want longer prison sentences, and welfare mothers to go out and work. White America is tired of hearing about racism and says 'We've done enough.'"

In these times of racial and economic polarization, police

officers are increasingly in the line of fire, called upon to quell the growing antagonisms. Criminal justice solutions, however, are woefully inadequate to heal the deep social wounds that plague contemporary America.

Placing the black community under police siege will do little to facilitate the struggle for enlightened solutions. Instead, police violence "in the line of duty" will stir up more black anger. When that anger reaches the boiling point, we can expect to see more St. Petersburgs. That would mark the beginning of a downward spiral whose repercussions, rest assured, will not be limited to the inner cities.

| "*"Police racism' will diminish precisely as fast as the black crime rate does."*

The Police Are Not Racist

Michael Levin

Michael Levin argues in the following viewpoint that labeling every police-minority altercation as racist is unfair. He asserts that police have more encounters with black suspects because blacks commit a disproportionate number of violent crimes. Police use deadly force only when they are threatened by a suspect, he contends. Levin is a contributing editor for the Center for Libertarian Studies.

As you read, consider the following questions:
1. In Levin's view, why was Johnny Gammage shot by police?
2. What percentage of drivers who are stopped by New Jersey state troopers are black, according to Levin?
3. According to the author, how many more robberies, murders, and rapes do blacks commit compared to whites?

Reprinted from "Much Ado About Amadou," by Michael Levin, *Rothbard-Rockwell Report*, July 1999, by permission of the Center for Libertarian Studies, Burlingame, California.

The script is always the same. A black does something bad—by driving recklessly, robbing a candy store, assaulting someone or in some other way getting involved in an altercation. White policemen appear. The perpetrator or someone mistaken for him fails to heed an order to stop/show his hands/pull over/display his license. Often he draws a gun or, if in a car, tries to run over one of the cops. The police attempt to subdue him by force, injuring or killing him.

Police Action Is Unfairly Magnified

Within hours community leaders—translation: no visible means of support—organize demonstrations against "police brutality," complete with a telegenic chorus of black women wailing "they've got to stop killing our babies" even though the deceased was 6' 2" and weighed 250 pounds. These small protests acquire a life of their own under media magnification. Well-known blacks suddenly remember how often they have been hassled by the police for no reason, allegedly, other than their color. Politicians, to show "racial sensitivity," declare that a grave wrong was done.

After meeting with Jesse Jackson, the US attorney general announces "possible civil rights violations," a guarantee that the cops will face federal charges should they escape local ones. All sides agree that the only cure for the racism inherent in the police department is a double dose of race preference: more blacks on the force at all levels—necessitating easier qualifying exams—and fewer white cops in black neighborhoods.

Cases in point: Eleanor Bumpers, shot to death by a policeman she attacked with a knife when he tried to mediate a family dispute; Kiko Garcia, shot to death attempting to grab a cop's gun from his holster; Abner Louima, beaten during a 3:00 A.M. brawl outside a homosexual bar; Johnny Gammage, shot by highway patrolmen he attempted to run down; and of course Rodney King, stopped for speeding and drunken driving.

An Unfortunate Chain Reaction

One of the two most recent incidents involves Amadou Diallo, a Guyanese immigrant. At 1:00 A.M. in February 1999, four plainclothesmen from the elite Street Crimes Unit [SCU] spotted a man (Diallo) fitting the description of a wanted rapist as he loitered on a Bronx street. Leaping from their unmarked car they asked Diallo to stand still and show identification, triggering an unfortunate chain reaction. Instead of complying immediately, Diallo backed up and reached into his pocket; at that very moment one of the SCU men stumbled while another yelled "Gun!," causing all four to open fire with their service automatics. In a few seconds Diallo was dead.

A few seconds later community leader Al Sharpton was on the scene, demanding the cops be indicted for murder. A day or two later the usual suspects began marching in front of police headquarters—when someone had the bright idea of engaging in "civil disobedience." Pretty soon a dozen people had been arrested and taken a few feet to be booked (remember, the scene was police headquarters). Suddenly getting arrested at One Police Plaza became the In thing, and second-rate celebs began making the scene as if it were the latest hot restaurant. Ossie Davis, Susan Sarandon, Dick Gregory, and the redoubtable Jesse [Jackson] himself, along with more than a thousand others, were duly led away in handcuffs.

Things went less well for the four policemen. New York's Mayor Rudy Giuliani initially pleaded for suspension of judgment until the facts were in, but the media ridiculed his circumspection for "insensitivity" to blacks. As Diallo's parents thanked him on TV, the Bronx District Attorney indicted the policemen on charges of 2nd degree murder, punishable by life in prison.

A Guilty Suspect

The facts? For one, Diallo spoke little English and probably did not grasp the orders given him. More suggestive was the revelation, a few days after the shooting, that he was in the United States illegally; he had told the Immigration and Naturalization Service that he was a Mauritanean fleeing political persecution (a magic formula that opens all immigration doors).

So imagine his guilty thoughts when four white representatives of officialdom suddenly confronted him. "They know I lied; they're going to deport me. Maybe I can get away. [The cops tell him to stand still.] Uh-oh; maybe shoving my wallet at them will convince them I'm on the up-and-up." The cops, already fearful that they are dealing with an armed robber-rapist, think he is going for a gun. One yells, one falls, and all open fire.

More Black Criminals than White

As of June 30 [1995], close to 6.8 percent of black male adults in America were in jail or prison compared to less than 1 percent of white male adults.

This is a tragedy all right. But it's a tragedy spawned for the most part by a permissive system of social coddling in this country that has black ghetto thugs practically immune to old-fashioned standards of right and wrong.

It is not a tragedy, as some would claim, spawned by widespread racism among our American police.

Ken Hamblin, *Conservative Chronicle*, December 27, 1995.

But the particulars offer a too narrow view of the Diallo case. To understand it fully, consider a second racial melodrama now playing itself out, the charge of "racial profiling" currently being made against the New Jersey Highway Patrol [NJHP]. It seems that, while only 35% of the vehicles on NJ [New Jersey] roads are driven by blacks, more than 70% of the drivers stopped by state troopers are black. This statistical "discrimination"—to liberals, the worst sin—has prompted the usual commotion and calls for investigation.

Racial Melodrama

To check up on troopers in future, patrol cars are being equipped with videocams to record all traffic stops. (Consider the waste in having policemen watching tapes at headquarters instead of being out protecting life and property, their proper function.) A more immediate result was the firing by New Jersey's governor, at the behest of the NAACP [National Association for the Advancement of Colored People] and "Black Ministers Council of New Jersey," of the State Police Superintendent, Carl Williams. The reason: he did not go along with the feeble defense other NJ officials were offering of NJHP tactics.

These other officials had mostly led with their chins, making up lame excuses or denying the obvious. At first the NJHP kept insisting that its troopers did not single out blacks, and that cars are stopped for minor infractions like malfunctioning taillights—which hardly explains why blacks are stopped more often, unless (what nobody had the guts to say) blacks are more neglectful of their cars. A TV station then produced an embarrassing patrolman's guide for a NJ township in which cars flying Ethiopian flags were described as likely to be transporting drugs.

Seeking to inject a note of realism into the debate, Williams called it "naive" to separate the race issue from crime. "Two weeks ago the president of the United States went to Mexico to talk to the president of Mexico about drugs. He didn't go to Ireland. He didn't go to England. [Today] the drug problem is cocaine or marijuana. It is most likely a minority group that's involved with that."

A Perfectly Proper Response

Certainly, drugs should be legal; trafficking is so lucrative and the cause of so much crime only because drugs are now illegal. State troopers shouldn't be stopping anyone for drug searches. But this is beside the larger point, which is that *racial profiling is a perfectly proper response* to what even the staunchest libertarian will regard as criminal. Blacks commit a disproportionate amount of all forms of violence against persons and property. So long as society either privately or collectively is justified in using force against criminals (as of course it is), blacks will be disproportionately discomfited.

Per capita, blacks commit about ten times as many robberies, murders, and rapes as do whites. This disparity, usually chalked up to bias in the justice system, is also found in victim reports. And this disparity is one that all policemen are aware of. They are more suspicious of a black than they would be of a white in identical circumstances—driving oddly on the highway, being out in the wee hours—and it is perfectly reasonable for them to be so. As it turned out, the robber-rapist Diallo was mistaken for was subsequently ap-

Reprinted by permission of Steve Kelley.

prehended a few blocks from where Diallo was shot, and looks rather like him.

Nor is this a purely intellectual judgment that entitles the police to be more suspicious of blacks. Cops have also learned to be more apprehensive and more prepared for trouble when confronting blacks in a tense situation. In any confrontation violence is always close to the surface. And it is this general atmosphere rather than any particular gesture on Amadou Diallo's part which explains his death. Cops associate blacks with potential violence, so, out of sheer self-preservation, are more prepared to use violence in dealing with them. "Police racism" will diminish precisely as fast as the black crime rate does.

Police Paralysis

An immediate and entirely predictable consequence of the hysteria about the Diallo shooting was police paralysis. In the weeks after the incident arrests fell by 250% and the murder rate, down to 650 per year, began to creep back up to the 2000+ per year level it had reached under Giuliani's black predecessor, David Dinkins. The police were inhibited in their dealings with blacks by fear that one misstep could lead to *their* arrest. And, needless to say, most of the victims of the preventable murders that occurred as a result were themselves black.

Given that blacks are the main beneficiaries of an aggressive local constabulary, why do black leaders oppose it so frenziedly? Part of the answer may be different levels of tolerance for disorder; measures regarded by whites as necessary for social life are perceived by blacks as impositions. Part of the answer may be a failure to link cause to effect: a black sees white cops handcuffing other blacks, and simply fails to realize that he is safer as a result.

But the main reason for the opposition is tactical: it keeps whites off balance. It lets whites everywhere know that if they harm a black, their lives are over. This intimidation has its uses, the most conspicuous of which is making justice impossible. The Los Angeles riots [following the 1992 acquittal of white police officers accused of beating black motorist Rodney King in 1991] demonstrated to juries everywhere that blacks will run amok if they don't get the verdict they want. That is why OJ Simpson got off, and why the NY cops will spend at least twenty years in jail.

> "*[In Los Angeles] a dozen killings of mentally ill or unstable people over the past six years [between 1993 and 1999] came in confrontations involving questionable police tactics and use of deadly force.*"

Ineffective Training on Handling the Mentally Ill Causes Police Brutality

Los Angeles Times

The *Los Angeles Times* argues in the following viewpoint that many people with mental illness are on the streets due to a lack of community-based health clinics where they could receive help. In consequence, the newspaper maintains, the mentally ill come into frequent contact with police, and many of these encounters turn deadly because police have not been properly trained to deal with people who have mental illness. The newspaper contends that to decrease police brutality, police departments must provide their officers with more effective training in how to defuse potentially dangerous situations with the mentally ill. The *Los Angeles Times* is a daily newspaper serving the greater Los Angeles area.

As you read, consider the following questions:

1. According to the *Los Angeles Times*, how many mentally ill people were shot in the period from 1994 to 1999 in Los Angeles?
2. How many officers does the Memphis, Tennessee, police department train to handle dangerous situations with mentally ill suspects, according to the author?

Local jails have become the de facto warehouses of the severely mentally ill, and those who deal with the mentally ill in crisis are too often men and women who wear guns and badges.

Of course, it was not supposed to turn out this way. Those released from hospitals, and those who would once have been confined to such places, were to have been treated in community-based mental health clinics. These clinics were never built. Now, the cycle too often runs from the streets to arrest to jail and back to the streets.

Deadly Encounters

The jails and the police cry foul: This is not the kind of work that should have been dumped in their laps. Agreed. But this situation won't change in the foreseeable future. The police must become equipped to deal appropriately with the mentally ill, through better training and awareness. Los Angeles Police Chief Bernard C. Parks presides over a department whose officers have, since 1994, shot 37 people who were exhibiting irrational behavior or symptoms of mental illness. Twenty-five of those were killed.

Times writers Josh Meyer and Steve Berry report that a dozen killings of mentally ill or unstable people over the past six years [between 1993 and 1999] came in confrontations involving questionable police tactics and use of deadly force. The example we all know is the tiny homeless woman, Margaret Laverne Mitchell, killed in May 1999, by an officer who said he feared she would harm him with a screwdriver. Just as hard to understand is the death of the unarmed J. Pantera in Venice, California, who challenged officers after he threw a grapefruit at their car.

That's disturbing enough, but allegations have also surfaced about falsified police information that exaggerated the threat in some of these cases. However, in contrast with the complex Rampart police corruption scandal [in which several officers in the Los Angeles Police Department were charged with corruption in 1999], needlessly violent confrontations between police officers and the mentally ill can be clearly addressed through better training. Police officers can't be prepared to deal with the mentally ill through just a few hours of training or by a single video. The emphasis should be on negotiation and defusing a potentially dangerous situation so that guns are unnecessary.

Better Training Needed

The Memphis, Tennessee, Police Department trains about one in 10 of its officers in how to handle dangerous situations with mentally ill suspects. It's a cost-effective approach that uses training by mental health professionals at no cost to the city of Memphis. It's also a nationally recognized program that has spread to police departments in Portland, Albuquerque, Seattle and San Jose.

Tragic Mistakes

Imagine you're a police officer responding to a complaint about someone who's out in the street waving a knife. When you arrive on the scene, you can't tell if the person is drunk, drugged or simply intent on doing harm. The person fails to respond to your verbal commands, an officer's first line of defense. What do you do?

If you're like many police officers, you might not stop to think that the person may be mentally ill or emotionally disturbed, says San Francisco Police Department (SFPD) Sgt. Forrest M. Fulton, PhD, one of a handful of psychologists who are also sworn police officers. And that oversight can end in tragedy, says Fulton.

People in these states sometimes attack or even kill police officers. In other cases, officers have had to resort to lethal force after overestimating their ability to use rational persuasion with people who aren't in touch with reality.

Rebecca A. Clay, "More Police Opt for Psychology Training," www.apa.org, 1997.

Chief Parks, as well as city, county and mental health officials, should consider adapting such a program to the needs of Los Angeles. Better training will protect police as well as the mentally ill by teaching officers how to avoid development of dangerous situations. In so doing we might save the life of a future Margaret Mitchell.

When a wild animal is loose in Los Angeles, much thought usually is given to how to safely return it to the wild. The animal is shot only as a last resort, an occurrence that almost always generates public outrage. It's a shame that a mentally ill person here can't get at least as much consideration as a mountain lion.

✳ *"Across many cultures women police officers use force less frequently than their male counterparts . . . and are more likely than male officers to diffuse potentially violent situations."*

A Lack of Female Officers Causes Police Brutality

Tracy Fitzsimmons

In the following viewpoint, Tracy Fitzsimmons argues that in order to reduce police misconduct, police must integrate more women officers into their departments. She claims that moving from a male-dominated police force that is based on violence to a female-centered one based on negotiation is vital to ensure that police treat both suspects and the victims of crimes with respect. Fitzsimmons has done research on human rights and policing and now teaches government at the University of Redlands.

As you read, consider the following questions:

1. What percentage of all reported crime in Peru involves women beaten by their spouses, according to Fitzsimmons?
2. According to the author, what percentage of women in Pakistani police custody reported physical or sexual abuse by the police?
3. In Pakistan and Haiti, what percentage of rape victims never take their case to the police for fear of being stigmatized or assaulted?

Reprinted from "Engendering a New Police Identity?" by Tracy Fitzsimmons, *Peace Review*, June 1998, with permission from the author and publisher.

Around the globe, democratization and peacebuilding processes have been transforming security forces. From Haiti to Bosnia to South Africa, international agencies have been spending millions of U.S. dollars to try to professionalize and civilianize the police—to create accountable and representative police forces to reflect the emerging "democracies" and to replace often repressive pre-existing security forces. For women's rights activists, the dismantling and subsequent democratic rebuilding of old security forces is particularly critical, since those forces have so often committed rape and sexual torture against women.

Reforms Have Failed

But while the sexual violence has often been curtailed, efforts to reform the police further have fallen short. These reforms have mostly churned out new "civilianized" police forces that are accountable to only half the population—the male half. Over the last decade, peacebuilding efforts throughout Latin America, Eastern Europe and parts of Africa have produced new police forces but they count few women among their ranks and have received little specialized training on crimes against women.

Take, for example, the new Haitian police: the scant 7% of their new force who are female largely serve as desk officers and traffic cops. The four-month-long training course (run by a U.S. Justice Department agency) for all new Haitian police officers includes less than half a day on rape and domestic sexual violence, even though over 40% of the female population has reportedly experienced those crimes. Even the few countries that have tried to incorporate women into their police forces now appear to be backsliding: El Salvador's five-year-old reformed police force has already shown a decline of women on the force from 7% to under 6%.

The "Male Identity"

In some sense, this trend should not surprise us, since gender issues have been a very low priority for the countries affected by the wave of democratization and peacebuilding. With the notable exception of the Scandinavian countries, those countries—such as Britain, Canada and the U.S.—that have enjoyed more sustained periods of democracy and peace have still fallen considerably short of producing police forces that respond to women. Many equate "gendering" se- ✳ curity forces with "changing the internal composition" of the police. But just as incorporating blacks into the South African police force in the 1980s did not make apartheid-era policing more responsive to black concerns, "gendered policing" must change more than just the gender composition of the police forces. It must also reform the way police departments, as institutions, treat women officers and victims of crimes against women. These reforms must alter the "male" identity of the police institution.

There are few places in the world where the mention of "police officer" does not conjure up the image of a man in uniform. If we analyze police systems around the world, we find: men protecting men from men, in accordance with laws designed by men. While this oversimplifies, the police (and law enforcement, more generally) unmistakably favors men. Radical feminists go even further, arguing that the police constitute a domain that also favors "male" characteristics—aggression over compromise, physical strength over finesse, and sexualizing over professionalizing the workplace. For these critics, gendering the police means not only integrating women cops and education about crimes against women, it also means changing the internal police environment, officer attitudes, and relationships across police ranks.

Women Officers Use Less Force

How can integrating women cops into police forces help buttress peacekeeping efforts? Whether under communist or capitalist rule, the old police and internal security forces were often among the most repressive agents of state terror. Many citizens lived in daily fear of their violence. As such countries move towards more democratic governance, civilianizing their security forces constitutes a key prerequisite for achieving peace. Since the police represent the state institution with which citizens most interact, policing provides an important indicator of how fairly the new government treats its citizens and how well a society can get along. When reformed or re-created police forces start to beat or harass citizens, social peace is probably on shaky ground.

While creating civilized and non-violent police forces is crucial to peace-keeping ventures, gendering those forces takes peacebuilding one step further: it offers increased possibilities of domestic security and peace. International research shows that across many cultures women police officers use force less frequently than their male counterparts, are less authoritarian when interacting with citizens and lower-ranking officers, have better communication and negotiation skills, and are more likely than male officers to diffuse potentially violent situations.

Among new police forces, these studies are borne out in practice. In Haiti, for example, an entirely new police force replaced the old security force after the U.S. restored President Jean-Bertrand Aristide to power. After the new Haitian police's first six months, the Inspector General's (IG) office was already overwhelmed with complaints about police misconduct. But not a single one of those cases was filed against a woman officer. Nor had the IG received any complaints of improper use of force or firearms by women officers, as compared to several male officers who were so charged.

Domestic Abuse

Employing women as police officers also helps maintain another type of "domestic" peace—that within the household. For women around the world, surviving domestic battering and sexual abuse is often their primary concern. Their fears often increase when civil strife comes to an end. Demobilized guerrillas or government soldiers find themselves jobless, and they often abuse their partners to express their economic frustrations and to maintain their authority. In Peru, 70% of all reported crime involves women beaten by their spouses. In Japan, Tanzania and Sri Lanka, over 55% of women report physical or sexual violence by a domestic partner or intimate.

While some women may choose family or religious mediation to stop the violence, others may turn to the state for help. Therefore, how the police respond to crimes against women potentially affects a substantial portion of the population. Studies done in India, the U.S. and the Netherlands show that women police officers respond more effectively to violence committed against women, and are more likely to take action against domestic abuse. Thus, those who fear their spouses will more likely fare better as the number of women police officers increases. Yet before women are willing to apply for policing jobs or to report incidents of domestic violence, the police as an institution must be "approachable"—it must shed its traditionally "male" identity.

Male Turf

Besides being more representative and perhaps less violent, police forces that shed their "maleness" can also better overcome several related identity conflicts. Because men officers often view themselves as the rightful occupants of police jobs and view women cops as trespassers, the simple integration of women into police forces can produce hostilities when the two sexes are expected to work together. As women begin to "invade" what was traditionally male turf, men officers often view them as the unwanted "other"—and they make their unwelcome clear.

For example, in Haiti, men officers frequently refuse to patrol with women partners, or to share sources or leads with them. In the U.S., many of the first women officers were routinely sent out alone to patrol dangerous areas. And in India, male supervisors routinely segregate women police officers to safer and more "feminine" jobs such as handling juvenile cases or human relations. Such discrimination, sometimes overt and at other times more subtle, can decrease police effectiveness in preventing and investigating crime. More extensively gendering the police—beyond merely introducing women onto the force—can help minimize such internal conflict and lead to greater sharing of information and responsibilities among men and women police officers.

Perpetrators or Protectors

If the police can successfully shed their "male" identity, it may also affect state-society relations. Citizens under repressive regimes in the 1970s and 1980s learned to fear and distrust their governments—your supposed protector could easily become your aggressor. Such distrust of authority does not wane quickly. A pressing question in societies now attempting to build peace and democracy is how the citizens view the new state. Since the police constitute the state entity with which citizens often have the most daily contact, reforming societies now have to ask: how do citizens identify the new police—as perpetrators or protectors?

Women Reduce Police Brutality

National and international research shows conclusively that increasing the numbers of women on police departments measurably reduces police violence and improves police effectiveness and service to communities. The studies also show that women officers respond more effectively than their male counterparts to violence against women, which accounts for up to 50% of all calls to police. Yet this record stands in stark contrast to women's dramatic under-representation in police departments where they make up 13.8% of sworn officers nationwide.

Study after study shows that women officers are not as likely as their male counterparts to be involved in the use of excessive force. As a result, the under-representation of women in policing is contributing to and exacerbating law enforcement's excessive force problems. The actual and potential liability for cities and states is staggering, with lawsuits due to excessive force by male law enforcement personnel costing millions of dollars of taxpayer money every year.

National Center for Women and Policing, *The Status of Women in Policing*, 1998.

Thus, there should be no doubt about the peacebuilding potential of integrating women and gendered education into police forces. Under recent authoritarian regimes in Haiti and Bosnia, women (far more than men) were systematically subjected to politically or ethnically motivated sexual violence by the police and military forces for years. In the former Czechoslovakia, the secret police often coerced family members or friends to inform on a woman, which often led to the woman being interrogated or sexually abused by the police. And in 1993, more than 70% of women in Pakistani police custody reported physical or sexual abuse. These were police forces composed entirely or almost entirely of men.

Women Distrust Police

Although the governments have since changed in these countries, along with some police personnel and doctrines, we should not be surprised that women still distrust the new police forces. Women's trust will not come until they can be assured that the new police will be accountable to citizens of both sexes, and until the new forces represent women rather than exploit them.

Research shows a direct correlation between reducing the "male" identity of a police force and improving women's self-identity on that force. Occupation serves as a maker and reinforcer of identity, income, and societal norms. In other words, what one does often becomes the principal constructor of who one is. Therefore, when women reach a glass ceiling, or are placed within a glass cubicle, their self-worth and identity are directly affected. In Brazil, the police hire just enough women to fill the positions in specialized "women's stations" that focus solely on crimes against women; women have little or no career mobility outside those stations in the broader police hierarchy. While the stations themselves might be a step forward for gendered policing, the gendered division of labor is a step back.

Studies of women police officers in India show that the extensive job segregation by gender within its police forces only furthers women's self-doubts and reinforces their traditional cultural status as second-class citizens compared to men. When homicide, patrol, and internal investigations are no longer viewed as "men's domain," the self-identity of women police officers stands to improve dramatically.

Rape Often Not Reported

When parts (or all) of the state are seen as "male" or exclusive of women, it forces women back to the household. It pushes women to identify less with the public sphere and more with the private sphere; and it separates both spheres, rendering it less likely that women will report cases of sexual violence. For example, in Pakistan and Haiti, 80% of rape victims never take their case to the police. That is accounted for by the social stigma attached to being raped and by the police's routine refusal to record such complaints, often verbally assaulting or blaming the victim instead. Therefore, women tend to keep their problems and victimization to themselves—at home. If there are few women in law enforcement, or if women do not see the police as "approachable," women will continue to see their problems and their place as part of the private sphere—a place, as they learned under previously repressive regimes, that will likely be safer, anyway.

Of course, gendering the police while resolving the above identity conflicts may create a different crisis of identity—for men and for the police as the protective arm of the state. For many, "de-maling" the police amounts to destroying their ability to punish criminals and uphold justice; yet this is not true. Men have historically been identified as social-control managers and citizen protectors; many men are unwilling to share those responsibilities with women. Male cops often view gender reforms as placing them in the losing position of a zero-sum identity game. As women's roles and issues gain legitimacy among the police, male officers often translate women's gain as a loss of their own power and self-identity on the force and in the greater society.

Engineering a New Identity

Timing and impetus are crucial. Engendering a police force at its founding or during significant reforms can minimize this zero-sum identity game. If gendered policing can be introduced before the police force and its "masculine" identity are established, then the entrance of women and gender issues will less likely be perceived as lost identity and power for the male officers. Thus, there are mutual interests—not an ensured loss—in engendering a new identity for the police. Such benefits extend not only to the women police officers, but also to male cops, the police institution at large, and the peacebuilding process more generally.

The logic of gendering the police while also broadly reforming it stands in stark contrast to current practice. International funding agencies now appear to assume that if they can successfully professionalize and civilianize the police forces they are training, then this will inevitably lead to changes toward gendered policing. But, as we can see from examining the many police systems in existence throughout the world, the one does not inevitably lead to the other—and may in part exclude the other. The longer a "male" identity is allowed to become embedded in a police system, the more difficult it becomes to engender change in that system.

External Forces

Unfortunately, during the recent period of democratization and peacebuilding, a gendering process has not accompanied the creation of new police forces. Where civil society groups already existed, they have not given gender any priority but rather have focused largely on rectifying past injustices. Likewise, the international community tends to limit its peacebuilding to demilitarization, and its democratization to holding elections.

Yet since change that threatens an institution's identity and leadership is not likely to come from within, the impetus for gendered policing must come from forces external to the police. Domestically, women's and human rights groups must begin to see gendered policing as a social justice issue that should be on their agendas. Internationally, the United Nations and other agencies must integrate women's issues into their peacebuilding efforts. Like police forces, peacebuilding and democratization should be consciously gendered, not left to be segregated or "male." In the future, policies must be designed to engender these new police forces, while accounting for cultural and contextual differences.

If citizens view state agents and institutions as "masculine" or exclusive or unaccountable, it can profoundly affect whether women identify themselves or are treated as equal citizens within the emerging democracies. It may also influence the long-term success of peacebuilding efforts. Thus, rather than merely reflecting social inequalities and injustices, police reforms can serve to help change them.

Periodical Bibliography

The following articles have been selected to supplement the diverse views presented in this chapter. Addresses are provided for periodicals not indexed in the *Readers' Guide to Periodical Literature*, the *Alternative Press Index*, the *Social Sciences Index*, or the *Index to Legal Periodicals and Books*.

Steve Berry and Josh Meyer	"Mistakes Seen in LAPD Shootings of Mentally Ill," *Los Angeles Times*, November 11, 1999. Available from Times Mirror Square, Los Angeles, CA 90053.
Paul Chevnigny	"The Too-Secret Police," *New York Times*, March 26, 1999.
Johnnie Cochran Jr.	"Johnnie Cochran Takes on the LAPD," *Los Angeles Magazine*, December 1995.
Tessa DeCarlo	"Why Women Make Better Cops," *Glamour*, September 1995.
Dianne Freely and David Finkel	"Organizing for Accountability," *Against the Current*, November/December 1999.
Ken Hamblin	"Police Used as Fall Guys in Fight Against Crime," *Conservative Chronicle*, December 27, 1995. Available from PO Box 37077, Boone, IA 50037-0077.
Bob Herbert	"Breathing While Black," *New York Times*, November 4, 1999.
Noelle Howey	"Good Women, Bad Cops," *Mademoiselle*, October 1999.
John Kifner	"Police Account Is Challenged in Killing of a Troubled Man," *New York Times*, October 4, 1999.
Elizabeth Kolbert	"The Perils of Safety," *New Yorker*, March 22, 1999.
John McCormick	"A Top Cop in the Cross Hairs," *Newsweek*, July 5, 1999.
John O'Sullivan	"Black and Blue," *National Review*, April 19, 1999.
Christain Parenti	"Robocop's Dream," *Nation*, February 3, 1997.
Elaine Rivera	"The Police and the EDP's," *Time*, September 13, 1999.
Jack E. White Jr.	"Endangered Species: The Police Component in Black-on-Black Crime," *Time*, March 1, 1999.

CHAPTER 3

Do Modern Police Methods Cause Police Misconduct?

Chapter Preface

Videotaping, interactive websites, cell phones, and desktop publishing are all tools used by the "electronic posse," a term coined by the journal *Governing* to describe people who are willing to do something about the crime in their neighborhoods. Residents in a town in Massachusetts, for example, videotaped the prostitutes and drug dealers who were taking over their neighborhood; within six weeks, the criminals had fled.

Citizens in the electronic posse usually work in conjunction with police through community policing programs. Community policing aims to prevent crime before it happens by encouraging law enforcement officers to help residents patrol their own neighborhoods. William D. Eggers and John O'Leary, authors of a book about community policing, argue that "restoring public safety demands a renewed partnership between the police and the community." Advocates maintain that in addition to decreasing crime rates, community policing decreases cases of police brutality because it establishes a trusting bond between police and citizens.

Opponents of community policing argue that it doesn't guarantee a decrease in crime rates. Tucker Carlson, who writes for the *Weekly Standard*, claims that the community policing program in New Haven, Connecticut, actually led to an increase in crime because the police chief protected neighborhood criminals to the extent that he impeded the crime-fighting efforts of the force. He responded to critics by claiming that "the primary threat to public safety came not from criminals, but from police officers." Other critics argue that community policing increases cases of police brutality because cops walking a beat are watched less closely by the department and are more tempted to abuse the rights of perceived troublemakers.

The electronic posse and community policing programs are two of the strategies used by police departments today to fight crime. The authors in the following chapter examine whether community policing and other police methods are effective at reducing crime and decreasing policy brutality.

"Glee [over aggressive policing] has come at a cost to civil rights and liberties."

Assertive Policing Leads to Police Misconduct

Clarence Page

In the following viewpoint, Clarence Page maintains that the high-profile police brutality case involving Abner Louima has brought to light the systematic abuse within the New York City Police Department (NYPD). He asserts that the NYPD's "tough-on-crime" policies—where police arrest people for minor crimes like subway turnstile jumping—have resulted in out-of-control police officers who target innocent people. The NYPD needs to work with the community it serves, not against it, he argues, in order for crime rates and police brutality cases to decline. Page is a columnist for the *Chicago Tribune*.

As you read, consider the following questions:

1. According to Page, what are the basic tenets of the "broken windows" approach to preventive policing?
2. How much did civilian complaints against police use of excessive force rise in the period from 1993 to 1995, according to the author?
3. In the author's view, who are most often the victims of crime?

New York City Mayor Rudolph Giuliani insists that the shocking case of Abner Louima is isolated. The mayor is in deep denial and his denial only encourages more abuses.

Louima, a 30-year-old Haitian immigrant and part-time security guard, was gravely injured inside a New York City police station on August 9, 1997. One or more police officers sodomized him with a stick reported to be a toilet-plunger handle. Then the stick was jammed into his mouth, breaking his teeth.

Systematic Abuse

There is a lesson here for the rest of the nation. In response to the national uproar, the mayor took admirable steps, including a full investigation and town hall meetings between local residents and every one of the city's police officers. But if the mayor had paid more attention to the systemic nature of the problem, he might not now find himself searching for systemic solutions.

Until Louima, Giuliani dismissed calls to crack down on complaints of police misconduct. He argued that the complaints are the result of more arrests and his more assertive "zero-tolerance" assault on quality-of-life offenses.

His pride was showing. Giuliani had become the nation's most prominent advocate of the "broken windows" approach to preventive policing. The nickname comes from a 1982 *Atlantic Monthly* article, "Broken Windows: The Police and Neighborhood Safety," by James Q. Wilson and George L. Kelling, which later was expanded into a book titled *Fixing Broken Windows.*

Broken Windows

Its basic tenets are increased physical presence of police on the streets and a reduced tolerance for vagrants, graffiti, broken windows and turnstile jumping. When left unfixed, these early signs of incivility lead to more serious social decay, the authors assert.

Such aggressive policing has helped crime drop to 30-year lows in New York City (and most other major cities) during the three Giuliani years [1994 to 1997]—a drop that former Mayor David Dinkins is quick to point out began during his administration in 1992.

But Big Apple glee has come at a cost to civil rights and liberties. The *New York Times,* among other publications, featured profiles on middle-class New Yorkers of all races forced to spend a night in jail without charges on petty offenses in the name of "zero-tolerance" policing. Civilian complaints against police for excessive force rose by 61.9 percent in 1995, compared to 1993. Abuse-of-authority allegations went up by 86.2 percent. Allegations of illegal searches soared by 135 percent.

This Modern World by Tom Tomorrow. Used with permission.

Dinkins, writing in the August 26, 1997, *Village Voice,* argues that aggressive policing is not the cause of increased complaints. Most of the complaints "come from people who were not only not arrested, but not even ticketed," he writes. "Clearly, complainants are largely innocent bystanders who get caught up in illegal police behavior."

Louima claimed that one of the police officers shouted,

"It's Giuliani time, not Dinkins time" while attacking him. With that, the story became deeply partisan and political. Many believed the alleged statement to be a reference to Giuliani's get-tough attitude toward crime, compared to his predecessor, who outraged many cops by instituting a civilian review board for police misconduct complaints.

Giuliani's critics assert that the numbers would have soared even more had so many citizens not lost faith in the civilian review board, whose staff Giuliani tried to slash before the City Council blocked him.

Getting in Touch

Is there a middle ground between runaway criminals and runaway police? There is, but too often it is ignored in the heat of talk-show arguments and political disputes.

Sensational brutality cases like Louima's unfortunately polarize the issue between middle-class suburbanites who are angry and frightened of crime and low-income urban residents who catch most of the bad end of police behaving like occupying troops. That's tragic, because poor people are most often the victims of crime and have the greatest reason to cooperate with police in crime-fighting efforts.

That's what Kelling, the Rutgers University professor who helped develop the "broken-windows" idea, and his crime scholar partner Wilson had in mind all along, he told *Time* magazine. "Zero tolerance and 'sweeps' are not part of my vocabulary," he said. Rather, he said, his concept should be carried out in the context of a larger strategy of community policing, in which cops are encouraged to get out of their squad cars and involve themselves with community problems.

That comprehensive approach—getting in touch, not just getting tough—has worked to reduce crime, along with police misconduct complaints, in cities across the country. Los Angeles, whose aggressive policing became notorious during the Rodney King beating case, revamped its training and found that, lo and behold, crime went down.

So, yes, it is Giuliani time. It is time for Giuliani, among others, to send a new message to his police, a message that aggressive policing should work with local residents, not war with them.

> *"The police got tough on 'quality-of-life'*
> *offenses like blasting a radio or panhandling.*
> *In the process, they made New York's streets*
> *nicer places for the law-abiding."*

Assertive Policing Reduces Crime

Mona Charen

Mona Charen argues in the following viewpoint that critics of the New York City Police Department's (NYPD) assertive police methods tend to see racism where none exists. One high-profile case of police brutality is not an indication of widespread abuse, she maintains. Charen claims that assertive policing—the aggressive policing of quality-of-life crimes such as public drinking and graffiti-writing—has lowered crime rates in New York City and actually decreased the number of police shootings. Mona Charen is a nationally syndicated columnist.

As you read, consider the following questions:

1. How much have murder rates declined on the Lower East Side since 1994, according to the author?
2. According to the author, how many suspects died at the hands of police in 1998?
3. What is "Compstat," according to Charen?

Reprinted from "Hooray for the NYPD," by Mona Charen, *Conservative Chronicle*, March 21, 1999, by permission of Mona Charen and Creators Syndicate.

The race hustlers, hate mongers and assorted leftovers from failed city administrations past are ganging up on Mayor Rudy Giuliani of New York. Even some Hollywood celebrities, like Susan Sarandon, are showing up to have themselves arrested outside the mayor's office, along with the usual suspects, the Rev. Jesse Jackson, [civil rights leader] Al Sharpton and former New York City Mayor David Dinkins.

The putative reason for their protest is the mistaken shooting of African immigrant Amadou Diallo by four New York policemen [in February 1999]. The true reason for their protest is a desire to stigmatize and therefore reverse the most amazing urban turnaround since the great Chicago fire of 1871.

Urban Peace

The miracle that the Giuliani administration has wrought in New York City is so dramatic that it has stunned even those who planned it. As John Podhoretz details in the *Weekly Standard*, the city's overall crime rate has been cut in half in just five years—with minority neighborhoods benefiting the most. On the Lower East Side, the murder rate has dropped 81 percent since 1994, burglaries are down 72 percent, and rapes have declined by 60 percent. The numbers are comparable in other formerly hazardous neighborhoods.

The drop in crime, petty and serious, is not, as the Giuliani critics would have it, a mere artifact of a booming economy and a drop in the teenage population. As former Police Chief William Bratton and William Andrews argue in the spring edition of the *City Journal*, New York has maintained an unemployment rate of between 8 percent and 10 percent in the period between 1993 to 1999. That's double the national average. And the teenage population has remained steady, except among minorities, where it rose.

Nor has this urban peace been purchased at the price of a police reign of terror. Though the police department has been expanded by 3,000 officers since 1991, police shootings have declined. In 1995, the police used their guns 344 times. By 1998, the number had declined to 249. And fatalities in police shootings have dropped, too. In 1996, 30 of the shootings resulted in death. In 1998, 19 died at the hands of the police.

There are a few key race hustlers in New York, most notably Al Sharpton, who can stoke the tiniest spark of misunderstanding into a raging flame of racial animosity. Sharpton came to national attention by appointing himself an "adviser" to hoaxer Tawana Brawley [a fifteen–year–old girl who claimed to be the victim of a vicious racial crime committed in 1987 in New York. In 1988, a grand jury concluded that the story was a hoax.]. He went on to incite a near riot in Harlem at a shop owned by a Jewish merchant. Someone took the bait and torched the place, killing an innocent man. And Sharpton shows up whenever he sees a chance to encourage race hatred—his most recent contribution was persuading Abner Louima, the black man brutalized by New York police in 1997, to say that the cops had said, "It's Giuliani time!" before inflicting their torture. (This was later unmasked as a total fraud.)

Quality of Life

The revival of the New York Police Department [NYPD] was no fluke. As Bratton and Andrews make clear, the department was reorganized from top to bottom by the Giuliani administration. Cops were taken out of their patrol cars and put back on the streets. Computers were enlisted to keep track of where crimes were occurring, and these data were cross-referenced with information about the whereabouts of parolees.

Stop-and-frisk operations netted thousands of illegal

guns, and the police studiously denied criminals their infrastructure by going after fences, chop shops, auto exporters and prostitution customers. Precinct commanders were given more authority, and Compstat, the information gathering system, helped them target high-crime areas. Most famously, the police got tough on "quality-of-life" offenses like blasting a radio or panhandling. In the process, they made New York's streets nicer places for the law-abiding and nabbed a good number of serious criminals along the way.

Naysayers

The Sharptons and David Dinkins of the world were happier when New York was overrun by "squeegee men" [hustlers who clean windshields for money as motorists sit at stop lights] extorting cash from motorists, drug dealers strutting the streets unafraid, and teenagers openly swigging beer and vaulting over subway turnstiles. They liked a New York with 4,500 shootings a year.

But most New Yorkers are delighted with the change Giuliani has wrought. The mistaken shooting of an innocent man is a tragedy. But to undo the great work of the NYPD in the name of Diallo would be a crime.

| "*[Community policing] will give the police more ability to use crime against the people, enabling them to direct it against people who oppose them and spare the ones who cooperate.*"

Community Policing Does Not Prevent Police Brutality

Revolutionary Worker

In community-based policing, a community's residents and its institutions work with police to reduce crime and police brutality. In the following viewpoint, the *Revolutionary Worker* argues that community policing will not reduce crime or prevent police misconduct. The police need crime in order to justify their existence, the newspaper contends, and furthermore, they rely upon force and brutality to suppress minority youth and the poor. In addition, the newspaper asserts, community policing turns participating civilians and institutions into paramilitary forces that are used to oppress the very people who most need protection. The *Revolutionary Worker* is a weekly newspaper published by the Revolutionary Communist Party.

As you read, consider the following questions:

1. What were "Judenrats," according to the *Revolutionary Worker?*
2. According to the newspaper, what happened to Gidone Busch?
3. In the newspaper's view, whom do the police "serve and protect"?

Reprinted from "The Trojan Horse of Community-based Policing," editorial, *Revolutionary Worker*, October 10, 1999, available at www.mcs.net/~RWOR, by permission of RCP Publications. Greenhaven editors have changed and/or added subheads to this article.

Advocates of community-based policing [CBP] say they want "cooperation instead of confrontation" between the police and the inner-city communities. They say that this will cut down both on police murders of innocent people as well as the ongoing, daily harassment of people of color. At the same time, they claim that CBP will reduce the crime that dogs the people in oppressed neighborhoods.

Eyes and Ears of the Police

But how does this "cooperation" work in practice? Basically, CBP aims to turn people in the oppressed neighborhoods into the eyes and ears of the police. The San Diego chief of police put it this way: "Our basic premise is, we don't have enough police officers to do it all, so we need community participation." CBP does this in several ways.

First, CBP gets the police involved in delivering basic social services. In Fort Wayne, according to the *New York Times*, "The city is divided into 227 neighborhoods, each with an assigned police officer who has the authority to call on city agencies like the parks department or the housing code department." The police chief there says that this gives the police a "constant flow of tips." No doubt. Control over services like housing and recreation enables the police to groom a handful of flunky types with the perks at their disposal, while holding the denial of such services over the heads of everyone else.

Second, CBP enlists "volunteers." San Diego has recruited 1,200 of them. According to the *Times*, "Many of them [are] retired people who receive police training, wear police-like uniforms and drive around in official vehicles. They help watch their neighborhood or work on police department computers so officers can patrol." Such volunteers can form a pro-police paramilitary force embedded in the neighborhoods. In cities like San Diego, right on the border, these volunteers are a potential vigilante force against immigrants.

Third, since the people rightfully have very little trust in the police, CBP tries to enlist institutions that the people do trust. Both Bill Clinton and a June 1, 1998, *Newsweek* article applauded police-clergy cooperation in Boston. There a team of ministers turn over some youth to the police—in return, they say, for "having a chance to turn around" the rest. Some of the ministers involved have taken good stands in the past; but in the name of "saving youth from gangs," and in return for access to dollars for social service programs, they've now become an arm of the police and prison system. (This kind of deal calls to mind the "Judenrat" in Nazi-occupied Poland—councils of "respectable" Jews who were allowed to decide which Jews would go to the concentration camps first, in return for keeping the ghetto quiet. The Judenrat councils were strung along to the very end, and then finally they, too, got killed. If that analogy sounds extreme, then think about how extreme it is that almost two million people rot in U.S. prisons today—the most in the world, and the majority are people of color.)

Massive Snitch Network

In return for this "cooperation," the authorities promise two things: an end to rampant police brutality and a drop in crime. For reasons we'll get into shortly, they won't deliver on either of these promises. But just for the sake of argument, let's assume that CBP worked to do both those things. What then? Would CBP be worth it?

Absolutely not. CBP aims to build nothing less than a massive snitch network among the oppressed, glued together by bribes and intimidation. The purpose of this snitch network is to push further the criminalization of an entire generation and to suppress any kind of resistance to this program. The people must not collaborate with the armed enforcers of their own oppression: this is both an important moral principle and a basic rule of mother-wit.

First, on the mother-wit point: when has bringing in the police ever helped a situation? Did calling 911 help Tyisha Miller [who was shot and killed by police in Riverside, California, in December 1988]? Or take Gidone Busch in New York—this mentally disturbed man was murdered in August 1999 by six policemen who claimed that they could not otherwise subdue a man wielding a simple household hammer! Six average people with street sense and "people skills" could have probably chilled the man out or, at worst, taken away his hammer and gotten him help. The Stolen Lives Project documents dozens of emotionally disturbed people who died at the hands of the police called in to help them. As Carl Dix [national spokesman for the *Revolutionary Worker*] has pointed out, if you've got a problem and you call the cops, then you've got two problems.

Capitalists Control Society

But the moral principle is even more important. The youth in the oppressed neighborhoods are not "bad kids." They have been denied decent education and health care and their families have been hit by economic misery. Society tells these youth over and over again that they are worthless, that they have no future and they don't even deserve one. The decent jobs began leaving the inner cities 30 years ago; today the main opportunity lies in the illegal economy. On top of this, the police themselves channeled crime into these neighborhoods. It's no mystery why a kid would get caught up in the "thug life."

This didn't happen by accident, or because of "bad choices" by these youth or their parents. The cuts in education and health care, the racist images in the mass media, and the withdrawal of jobs: these all resulted from conscious decisions by the capitalists who control the economic and political levers of society. And now, in order to solve the problem of crime, people should cooperate with the armed enforcers of the very class that put them in this hell? We don't think so!

Of course, the advocates of CBP say that the snitch network would only be used to get the real hard-core criminals out of the neighborhood. But just who decides who is a criminal and who is a predator? Nowadays, the system says that a homeless man hustling to wash windows is a "predator" who must be arrested and even shot, while the real estate baron who uses arson and interest rates to drive poor people from their homes is a "role model." It declares that a youth who writes "Free Mumia" on a wall is a vandal who must be sent to prison, while the political hack who covered up racial profiling for six years in New Jersey gets a seat on the state supreme court. It decrees that immigrants seeking work are vicious outlaws to be hounded and even killed when they don't understand a command, while the ones who exploit them are "creative entrepreneurs." We need to get very clear on who the *real* criminals really are—and then decide whether CBP is a solution to our problem, or more of the same and worse.

Political Repression

Nor can we ignore the dimension of political repression in CBP. What if a neighborhood should organize to oppose the shutdown of a health clinic or a recreation center? What if someone goes so far as to tape or photograph police harassing or beating people? What do you suppose these "community-based" police, or their "volunteers," will do then? How do you suppose the cops would use their "constant flow of tips"?

We're not talking ancient history here. In New York, the police were caught in 1999 secretly videotaping meetings of students opposed to cuts in student aid. In Chicago, they held up and harassed 40 youth on their way to the October 22, 1998, demonstration, and they tried a similar trick in L.A. [Los Angeles]. Why on earth should we make it easier for them to spy on and suppress our movements? But that's exactly what CBP does.

CBP is a huge step to giving the police total control over our communities. Those of us in the movement to stop police brutality—those of us who have some hard-won sense of the real nature of the police—should *not* lend our support to any such measure. We should oppose it. And we should struggle with those in our movement who have been misled into taking up such a solution.

Cops Serve Only the Rich

Beyond the moral and political principle involved, CBP is a lot of bullcrap. For starters, CBP will not stop crime. This is because the job of the police isn't really to stop crime in the first place. Their job is to preserve order, which means the property relations of society. The cops "serve and protect" the rich and the super-rich against any threat to their property, whether it be criminals or people resisting their oppression. In regard to crime, the police keep some crimes away from the better-off areas, and use other crimes as ways of controlling the poorer, more proletarian areas.

Let's be real here—the police know who runs the drug trade, the chop shops, or whatever in any neighborhood. They manipulate the different crews against each other, and they ultimately decide who will operate and who will not. Sometimes the cops even get in on it themselves (though that kind of blatant corruption is actually not the main way that they are involved with crime). Their role is to regulate crime, not stop it. The police actually need a certain level of crime in the oppressed areas in order to justify their existence. If this dog-eat-dog and anything-for-money system didn't generate so much crime on its own, the cops would have to invent it.

Reduced Accountability

David Bayley, dean of the School of Criminal Justice at the State University of New York at Albany, says Chicago's community policing experiment has been the most heavily scrutinized model in the country. And while the experiment has shown promise so far, there are still countless ways it might fail. For one thing, unmotivated officers might find it easier than ever to slack off now that the department affords them time to get to know the neighbors and work out creative solutions to their problems. Out on patrol, they have fewer calls to answer and reduced accountability. Vigilante cops, meanwhile, might be more tempted to flout the rights of a perceived troublemaker if they feel they are working under less scrutiny and at the behest of community groups.

Jonathan Eig, *American Prospect*, November/December 1996.

You can see this in the way that the police in different cities have tried to break up the gang truces, even though these truces cut way down on the turf war murders of the late '80s and early '90s. Why would the police do that? Because the truce movement also cut down on the police control of things and could give people the idea that we might solve our own problems relying on ourselves.

You can see a similar thing in New York. As the economy opened up a little bit in the last few years, and as the drug trade stabilized and changed in character, crime began to go down. But arrests continued to go up, because Mayor Rudolph Giuliani ordered the cops to arrest people on the pettiest violations they could cook up!

If anything, the snitch network and volunteers of CBP will give the police more ability to use crime against the people, enabling them to direct it against people who oppose them and spare the ones who cooperate.

CBP Will Not Stop Brutality

The other big lie about CBP is that it will cut down on police brutality. First off, why should the police need a big snitch network in order to cease being brutal? What does one thing have to do with the other? Aren't they really saying "Look, we're subjecting people in your neighborhood to totally unjustified terror—but if you give us what we want, which is more information, we'll think about going easier on you"?

No advocate of CBP has ever answered this question, or even tried, so far as we know. But while there may be no excuse for police brutality, there is a reason. Shortly after the killing of Amadou Diallo [by New York City police officers in 1999], the newspapers quoted a social worker explaining why the police stop, frisk and harass so many young Black and Latino men for no reason:

> The worst experience you can have is a sense of total helplessness and a feeling you have to cower in the presence of somebody else. What's frustrating is, we hear that somehow this is for our own good. [They say] they're doing this to protect us and take care of the community. In the process . . . [they're] breaking the spirit . . . of a generation of young men. . . . [They're] breaking their will.

This system holds no future for the youth, especially for youth of color. No wonder the rulers find the will and spirit of this generation of black and other youth of color something to suppress. Police brutality is an indispensable weapon for doing that, and they are not about to give it up. For all the talk about "community-based policing," the formation and reinforcement of heavily armed SWAT teams goes on in almost every community. The hiring of police goes up, even as poor schools scramble for teachers and social services are cut yet again. The cops in New York killed seven people in August 1999, the Houston Police Department killed three more, and so it continues. People like Bill Clinton promote CBP in order to supplement the heavy hand of the police and make it more efficient, rather than replace it. We know why he does it—the question is why should WE?

The Trojan Horse

Our movement is only now beginning to catch fire. Many younger people have just begun to get a glimpse of the potential power of the people. For the first time in a generation, revolutionary collective solutions to social problems—solutions that rely on the people—are beginning to seem possible. Let's not make a terrible mistake and waste this potential.

At a time like this, we should remember the story of the Trojan horse. For years the armies of Greece laid siege to the ancient city of Troy. They used armed force, fire, and starvation against the Trojans. But nothing they did could break the will of Troy. Finally, the Greeks told the Trojans that they were giving up. Not only that, they said Greece would give Troy a gift in tribute to its fighting spirit: a huge wooden horse. The Trojans accepted this gift and began a great celebration of their victory. Finally, worn out from their merrymaking, the Trojans fell asleep. It was only then that the Greek soldiers snuck out of their hiding places in the massive wooden horse and slaughtered the now-defenseless inhabitants of Troy.

Our movement must reject the Trojan horse of community-based policing.

| *"In the coming years many more communities should adopt [community policing as a] highly effective, humane, and economical way to cut crime."*

Community Policing Reduces Crime

Edmund F. McGarrell

In the following viewpoint, Edmund F. McGarrell argues that community policing—in which police officers try to prevent crime before it happens by establishing trusting relationships with the people in the neighborhoods they serve—has helped produce a national decrease in crime rates. Police departments must reward officers for preventing crimes, he asserts, and provide them with more time to become acquainted with the people on their beat. McGarrell directs the Hudson Institute's Crime Control Policy Center and is chair of the Department of Criminal Justice at Indiana University.

As you read, consider the following questions:
1. According to McGarrell, what percentage of Spokane's drug arrests occurred in the West First Street neighborhood in 1994?
2. By the end of the second year of Project ROAR, what percentage of residents reported observable declines in drug-related crime and street prostitution, according to the author?
3. According to the author, how many citizen complaints were filed in response to a ninety-day patrol project in Indianapolis that resulted in sixteen hundred traffic citations?

Reprinted from "Cutting Crime Through Police-Citizen Cooperation," by Edmund F. McGarrell, *American Outlook*, Spring 1998, by permission of the author.

A major public policy surprise of the mid-1990s has been the significant decrease in crime in many major U.S. cities. Homicide rates in New York City, for instance, have fallen to a thirty-year low. There were fewer than 800 homicides in New York in 1997—compared to 2,262 in 1992. Los Angeles, Boston, New Orleans, Chicago, and Dallas have enjoyed similar declines. Although the trends have not reached all cities (exceptions include Denver, Detroit, Louisville, Nashville, and Indianapolis), the declines have been large enough to produce a national decrease.

Community Policing Cuts Crime

Analysts have offered many different explanations for the decrease, including the decline in crack cocaine wars, demographic shifts decreasing the number of males in crime-prone age categories, an improved economy, and increased levels of incarceration. Although they disagree about which factors are producing the decline—the real cause is probably a combination of factors—many if not most observers believe that the nationwide trend toward community policing has been a key ingredient.

Community policing means different things to different people, however, even among police themselves. Also, its operational manifestations differ from city to city and even between neighborhoods within a city.

Nonetheless, a close look at a community policing effort in a U.S. city reveals several distinct elements of this approach. It appears to be a humane and economical way of fighting crime. This effort and successful ones in other communities tell us what American law enforcement will look like in the future if we build on these contemporary success stories.

Drugs and Prostitution

Spokane, Washington, is a city of approximately 185,000 residents in a county of just under 400,000 population, in eastern Washington twenty miles from the Idaho border. It is the center of economic, cultural, and health resources for a very large rural area in eastern Washington, northern Idaho, and northwest Montana.

The early 1990s brought population and economic growth,

but also increases in violent crime, drug trafficking, and gang activity. Much of this illegal conduct occurred in the West First Street neighborhood, an older area on the edge of the downtown district. It is a mixed-use neighborhood zoned for commercial buildings, light industry, warehousing, and apartment buildings. It is also a poor neighborhood, with a median income approximately one-quarter that of the city as a whole; half its residents are below the poverty level. At the center of the neighborhood is a fifty-unit public-housing facility known as the Parsons. The neighborhood is traversed by a raised railroad line and numerous alleys and alcoves that have provided sites for much illegal activity. Commercial establishments included adult pornography arcades, taverns, and social service programs catering to runaway youth and drug users.

For many years the neighborhood was a "copping zone," a place to seek drugs and prostitution. In 1994, this approximately four-by-five-block neighborhood accounted for 13 percent of the city's drug arrests and 8 percent of its robberies while comprising much less than 1 percent of its population.

From late afternoon through the early morning hours a steady stream of cars and trucks drove through the neighborhood. A driver would place an order for drugs or sex to a street-side vendor, proceed to another block for payment, and move to the next stop to procure the product. The streets were dominated by lookouts, sellers, and buyers in these illicit markets.

Residents of the public-housing facility described themselves as prisoners within their apartments. Although happy with the facilities, they were afraid to leave them. More than 80 percent reported feeling unsafe in the neighborhood at night. The number for the rest of the city was 24 percent. One resident noted that she did not need cable TV because she could spend her evenings looking out her window and observe more illegal activity than she would ever see on TV.

Project ROAR

In the winter of 1994, public-housing residents, the Spokane police, the housing authority, local business owners, and a local church decided that conditions had become intolerable. They initiated a collaborative effort to reclaim the neighborhood—Project ROAR, for "Reclaiming Our Area Residences."

The police dedicated a neighborhood resource officer (NRO), who was relieved from responding to calls for service outside the neighborhood and directed to work with local residents and business owners to reduce crime and disorder and improve the quality of life. The housing authority contributed office space in the Parsons Building for a project coordinator to organize a resident association.

Business owners participated in regular problem-solving meetings convened by the neighborhood resource officer and provided resources for various crime prevention measures and neighborhood improvements. The public-housing residents formed a tenant association, participated in problem-solving meetings, and provided social activities. The goal was to bring residents out of their apartments, restore a sense of ownership over the neighborhood, and build a community.

Realizing that the traditional reactive police response to crime incidents had not reduced crime in the neighborhood, the NRO worked with other police in a variety of proactive strategies. Officers worked on foot and bicycle patrol to increase the visible police presence. Drug and gang units performed undercover work and periodic sweeps, and drug arrests tripled during the first two years. The police also sent letters to individuals observed driving through the neighborhood and conversing with suspected drug dealers and prostitutes, warning that the neighborhood was dangerous. The true intent, of course, was to notify potential vice customers that the police were aware of them.

Community and Police at Work

Police worked with businesses to implement environmental changes. They established no-parking and no-stopping areas to thwart the drive-throughs, and installed fences with gates on alley entrances. The fences allowed delivery vehicles to serve stores, bars, and restaurants during the day but closed the alleys during the night, eliminating a popular site for illegal business. Residents painted the areas under viaducts—a favorite location for drug deals and prostitution—and installed brighter lighting there and on the streets and in parking lots. They also placed surveillance cameras on several street corners.

Crime Reductions

Community policing, which makes citizens allies of the police, is thriving in many cities, from Chicago to San Diego and from Fort Wayne, Indiana, to Fort Worth, Texas. Based on statistics alone, several of these cities have surpassed New York City in reducing crime. Where homicides in New York City have dropped by two-thirds from a record high in 1990, in San Diego they have dropped by three-fourths from their peak in 1991. Where New York City has seen a 41 percent decline in overall violent crime in the past decade, Fort Worth has recorded a 56 percent drop, according to a new study by the Justice Department.

Fox Butterfield, *New York Times*, April 4, 1999.

The police opened a mini-station in the Parsons Building, providing an office for the NRO and drop-in location for other police officers. The mini-station, staffed by neighborhood volunteers, became a center for crime prevention, neighborhood improvement, and social activities. Two community corrections officers moved in, facilitating supervision of neighborhood clients.

The residents performed a number of activities to address safety concerns and increase social cohesion. They formed watch committees and developed crime report forms so that they could report on illegal activities. They established a buddy system to took out for one another. They worked with the NRO to organize neighborhood marches and social activities including block parties, bingo nights, potluck dinners, and movie and music nights. Before Project ROAR, such social events were nonexistent; the average since has been above nine per month.

Dramatic Results

The various efforts elicited quite dramatic effects. Fear of crime in the neighborhood has dropped significantly. After one year, approximately 40 percent of the residents reported observable declines in drug-related crime and street prostitution. By the end of the second year, more than 70 percent reported such declines. While robberies and burglaries increased in a comparison neighborhood and held steady citywide, in the project area they declined 40 percent in the first two years. When the project began, 14 percent of the residents said that they were satisfied living in the neighborhood; by the end, more than 60 percent did and 90 percent were at least "somewhat satisfied." Residents' favorable opinions of the police rose from 55 to 89 percent.

Project ROAR involved three elements: proactive law enforcement, crime prevention, and community building. The glue binding these elements was the police-community partnership.

Proactive Enforcement

Community policing is not a retreat from law enforcement; it is simply a move from purely reactive policing to a proactive approach using problem-solving principles. It addresses crime through ongoing analysis, response, assessment, and action. West First Avenue, for instance, was an obvious "hot spot" of crime in Spokane, and the community worked to make the area uncongenial for buyers and sellers of drugs and prostitution.

In New York City, under former commissioner William Bratton, the police implemented a crime analysis program known as *compstat* (computerized analysis of crime statistics). Using computers to identify geographic crime patterns, command staff pinpoint criminal hot spots and craft strategies for addressing them. Police departments in Indianapolis, New Orleans, and other cities are implementing similar programs.

In these and other such programs, police no longer wait until an offense has occurred but actively study crime patterns, craft responses, and evaluate their interventions.

Prevention

Most such programs target specific types of crime and change the environment to make them more difficult, riskier, and less rewarding. These efforts have cut crimes as varied as car theft, burglary, and obscene phone calls. The security cameras, fencing of alleys, and similar measures in

Spokane reflect these "target-hardening" approaches.

An important element is to intervene quickly after an offense. Indianapolis, for example, has implemented a major experiment involving the use of restorative justice conferences for juvenile offenders. The program diverts youth offenders aged ten through fourteen from the juvenile court into restorative justice conferences. A youth faces the victim(s) of the offense, and both offender and victim are accompanied by family and friends. A trained facilitator, typically a police officer, leads a discussion of the harm that was done and the steps needed to restore justice.

The conference ends with an apology and restitution to the victim, community service, or other mutually agreeable actions. The conferences confront youths with the harm they have done and hold them accountable in a supportive setting, and also meet the victims' psychological and material needs. Local schools have begun to use similar conferences to address disciplinary problems.

Building Community

Early in this century, University of Chicago criminologists noticed that certain neighborhoods continually produced the most crime and social problems, even though the ethnic groups comprising them changed, whereas other neighborhoods remained relatively crime-free for decades. They theorized that high-crime areas were produced by social disorganization that shattered informal social controls, and thus that building communities was the surest way to cut crime. A 1997 study supports this thesis, indicating that neighborhood social cohesion is the strongest predictor of violent crime levels, even after controlling for poverty, residential instability, individual characteristics, and the like.

Community policing efforts such as Project ROAR build on these insights. Resident associations, social activities, and the like all aim at rebuilding the community.

Police-Community Partnership

Community policing is a partnership between the police and the citizenry. Open dialogue reduces friction and distrust, telling the police what the residents want and giving citizens the rationale behind police activities. Recently in Indianapolis, for example, citizens meeting with police officials called for increased enforcement in several neighborhoods plagued by violence and drug dealing. The police conducted a ninety-day directed patrol project after meeting with neighborhood residents and explaining their proposal. They enlisted widespread support, and although the project generated more than 8,500 traffic and pedestrian stops and 1,600 traffic citations, residents registered no complaints either formally or through the media.

Police Culture Must Change

The results from Spokane and many other communities show that neighborhoods can successfully use proactive law enforcement, prevention, and community building, based on a solid police-citizen partnership, to reduce crime. Future efforts, however, will confront certain organizational and conceptual issues that have yet to be resolved. These will shape the future of crime prevention.

Administrators, for example, will have to revise police organizations to implement these practices effectively. The modern police department—with its centralized, military structure—was designed to minimize corruption and efficiently respond to calls for service. Its structure and systems were not designed for innovation, creativity, and external relations, and in fact are somewhat antagonistic toward them. Officers trained, evaluated, and rewarded for reacting to crime understandably wonder whether community policing is real law enforcement.

Police departments must change that culture. They will have to give officers time to attend community meetings, keep them on assignments long enough to establish neighborhood ties, and reward them for solving neighborhood problems not "verified" by arrests or tickets.

Another question is whether this approach can work everywhere. Poorer neighborhoods with severe crime problems can be very difficult to organize. Recent evidence, including the Spokane project, suggests that police and citizens can establish successful partnerships in such neighborhoods, but we still have much to learn about how best to build and sustain these relationships and handle conflicts among competing factions.

Finally, we must learn more about the relationship between formal and informal control. Some political theorists—such as Simon Schambra—note that centralized governmental authority breaks down the informal socializing institutions of family and neighborhood. The Spokane project, however, and a 1997 study I participated in, suggest that formal social control may be a prerequisite for the informal kind: in high-disorder neighborhoods a sense of responsiveness from governmental institutions (local government and the police) decreased citizens' fear of crime. In low-disorder neighborhoods, it had no such effect; informal controls did the job. Ascertaining which neighborhoods need formal social controls will be a major element of crime control in the future.

Community policing experiments show that neighborhoods can successfully reduce crime by involving both residents and police in creating community and social order. That, of course, is a commonsense notion, and in the coming years many more communities should adopt this highly effective, humane, and economical way to cut crime.

> "*[Stops based on racial profiling] are arbitrary and unconscionable intrusions on the rights of New Yorkers who are supposed to be protected, not humiliated, by the police.*"

Racial Profiling Is Unjust

Bob Herbert

In the following viewpoint, Bob Herbert claims that racial profiling—stopping motorists simply on the basis of their race—is unjust because all people have a right to be in public places without being harassed. Herbert argues that racial profiling demoralizes its victims because it undermines their confidence in being treated equally under the law. The vast majority of those stopped by police, he maintains, are nonwhite and innocent. Herbert is a reporter for the *New York Times*.

As you read, consider the following questions:
1. What were Rossano Gerald and his son guilty of, in Herbert's opinion?
2. According to the author, how many people were stopped and frisked by the New York City Police Department in 1997 and 1998?
3. What was the purpose of the Chicago anti-loitering law, according to Herbert?

Reprinted, with permission, from "Hounding the Innocent," by Bob Herbert, *The New York Times*, June 13, 1999. Copyright ©1999 by The New York Times.

An anti-loitering law that allowed the Chicago police to arrest more than 42,000 people from 1992 to 1995 was declared unconstitutional in June of 1999 by the Supreme Court.

[Supreme Court justice] Antonin Scalia howled in dissent, which should tell you something. The law was an abomination, just like the practice in New York of stopping and frisking black and Hispanic people by the tens of thousands for no good reason. And just like the practice of pulling over and harassing perfectly innocent black and Hispanic motorists on streets and highways in many parts of the country.

The Faces of Ethnic Profiling

Ethnic profiling by law-enforcement authorities in the United States comes in many forms, and all of them are disgusting.

In the summer of 1998, sadistic members of the State Police in Oklahoma spent more than two hours humiliating Rossano Gerald, a 37-year-old Army sergeant, and his 12-year-old son, Greg.

Sergeant Gerald was pulled over and interrogated. He was ordered out of his car and handcuffed. The troopers asked if he had any guns. They asked permission to search the car and when he refused they searched it anyway. They separated Greg from his father and locked him in a police vehicle. They interrogated him. They brought drug-sniffing dogs to the scene. They dismantled parts of the car. When they finally tired of the madness, they told Sergeant Gerald he was free to go. No arrest was made. Greg, of course, was petrified. When the ordeal ended he wept uncontrollably.

Why did this happen? Greg and Sergeant Gerald were guilty of America's original sin. They were born black.

Profiling Targets the Innocent

In New York, profiling was not only perpetuated but elevated to astonishing new heights during the regime of [New York City mayor] Rudolph Giuliani. Here, the targets are mostly pedestrians, not motorists. Young black and Hispanic males (and in some cases females) are stopped, frisked and harassed in breathtaking numbers.

By the Police Department's own count, more than 45,000 people were stopped and frisked by members of the Street

Crimes Unit in 1997 and 1998. But the total number of arrests made by the unit over those two years was less than 10,000. And it is widely believed that the number of people stopped during that period was far higher than the 45,000 reported by the cops. The true number likely was in the hundreds of thousands.

Wasserman ©1999, Boston Globe. Distributed by Los Angeles Times Syndicate. Reprinted with permission.

Ira Glasser, executive director of the American Civil Liberties Union [ACLU], noted that two things characterize the New York City stops: "Virtually everybody is innocent, and virtually everybody is not white."

Mayor Giuliani, like most public officials, will not acknowledge that his police officers are targeting people by race. "The stops are driven by the descriptions of the person who committed the crime," Mr. Giuliani said.

Spare me. The vast majority of these stops are in no way connected to the commission of a specific crime, and the Mayor knows it. They are arbitrary and unconscionable intrusions on the rights of New Yorkers who are supposed to be protected, not humiliated, by the police.

Profiling Is Extensive

Most Americans have no idea of the extent of the race-based profiling that is carried out by law-enforcement officials, and the demoralizing effect it has on its victims. The ACLU, in a report called "Driving While Black: Racial Profiling on Our Nation's Highways," said: "No person of color is safe from this treatment anywhere, regardless of their obedience to the law, their age, the type of car they drive, or their station in life."

The Chicago law that resulted in more than 42,000 arrests over three years was aimed at curbing gang activity. It was clearly unconstitutional. It made it a crime for anyone in the presence of suspected gang members to "remain in any one place with no apparent purpose" after being told by the police to move on.

Why should one's purpose for being in a public place have to be apparent? As a reporter for *The New York Times*, I might be in the presence of a suspected gang member. What business is that of the police? And how could that possibly be a legitimate basis for an arrest?

The suit challenging the law was brought by the Chicago office of the ACLU. A spokesman for the group noted that the "vast majority" of the people arrested under the law were African-American or Hispanic.

What a surprise.

> "If drug traffickers are disproportionately black or Hispanic, the police don't need to be racist to stop many minority motorists."

Race Is an Important Consideration to Reduce Crime

Jackson Toby

Jackson Toby argues in the following viewpoint that current methods of apprehending drug traffickers are based on the theory that the best way to prevent major crimes is to target minor ones. Since statistics show that drug traffickers are disproportionately black or Hispanic, he maintains that regularly stopping minority motorists for offenses like speeding increases the likelihood that police will confiscate illicit drugs or weapons. Therefore, Toby claims, racial profiling is not racist, but practical. Toby, a professor of sociology at Rutgers University, was the director of the Institute for Criminological Research at Rutgers from 1969 to 1994.

As you read, consider the following questions:

1. According to Toby, by what percentage did felonies decline in the subways of New York City as a result of William J. Bratton's policing methods?
2. Why was Timothy McVeigh stopped by Oklahoma police, according to the author?
3. What percentage of suspects arrested for murder were black, according to Toby?

In February 1999, New Jersey Gov. Christine Todd Whitman forced the resignation of Col. Carl A. Williams, superintendent of the New Jersey State Police, for "insensitivity" because of remarks he had made in a newspaper interview. In replying to accusations that the state police targeted black motorists for traffic stops on the New Jersey Turnpike, Col. Williams had insisted that there was no racial profiling and that stops were made only "on the basis of a traffic violation."

Charges of Racism

However, he also was quoted by the *Newark Star-Ledger* as saying that certain crimes were associated with certain ethnic groups and that it would be naive to think that race was not an issue in drug trafficking. "Two weeks ago," Mr. Williams reportedly said, "the president of the United States went to Mexico to talk . . . about drugs. He didn't go to Ireland. He didn't go to England."

Responding to that statement, a group of black state legislators, ministers and civil-rights advocates gathered to denounce Col. Williams as a racist. "His views are dastardly," said New Jersey Assemblyman Leroy J. Jones Jr. "He's unfit to hold such a critical, important office." Mr. Williams was dismissed hours later.

The Williams comments, along with the 1999 New York City police killing of Amadou Diallo, an unarmed black man, have contributed to the impression of widespread police racism. But neither Mr. Williams nor the officers involved in the Diallo shooting had to be racist to say or do what they did. A little perspective is in order here.

Begin with one of the most important ideas in modern criminology, and one that has revolutionized police practice—the belief that a good way to prevent robberies, murders and other serious felonies is to go after minor offenses. Thus, when William J. Bratton was chief of the Transit Police in New York City from 1990 to 1992, part of his strategy for controlling violence in the subway system was to order his officers to crack down on small infractions—fare beating, panhandling, graffiti, smoking, boisterous behavior.

Within two years of the policy's adoption, the number of

felonies in the subway declined by more than 30%. Why? Well, one out of every six fare evaders stopped by the Transit Police in 1991 either was carrying a weapon or was wanted for another crime on an outstanding warrant. By paying attention to behavior that most people regard as not worth bothering about, the Transit Police prevented some violent crimes on the subways.

Racial Profiling Is Not Always Racist

Certainly much of what is made to seem racist behavior isn't.

Take the profiling of drug runners on the interstates. Police regularly stop, on any pretext, young black males in rental cars who are traveling between drug cities and don't have any vacation baggage.

From the police point of view, experience has shown that such young men are far more likely to be ferrying drugs than, say, blue-haired white couples driving campers.

Fred Reed, *Washington Times*, June 24, 1996.

The same principle applies to drug traffickers on the highways: People who violate major laws are probably also inclined to violate minor ones, such as traffic regulations. Consequently, stopping motorists for traffic violations has led to the seizure of major shipments of illegal drugs to Newark or New York—and even to the apprehension of a wanted murderer. The Oklahoma City bombing might have gone unpunished had the Perry, Oklahoma, police not stopped Timothy McVeigh because he did not have a license plate on his pickup truck.

A Civil-Liberties Cost

There is, of course, a civil-liberties cost to enlarging the police net. Cracking down on fare beaters on the New York subways snared (and embarrassed) passengers in a great hurry to get to appointments. Similarly, although the police have caught major drug traffickers by searching the vehicles of motorists stopped for traffic offenses on the New Jersey Turnpike, their success is counterbalanced by unsuccessful but intrusive vehicle searches of otherwise respectable citizens who made an illegal turn or drove faster than the speed limit. And a disproportionate number of those stopped were black or Hispanic. According to a survey sponsored by the New Jersey Office of the Public Defender, blacks accounted for 13% of drivers on the south end of the New Jersey Turnpike, 15% of speeders and 35% of those stopped by the state police.

Is this evidence of police racism? Not necessarily. True, most blacks and Hispanics are law-abiding. But if drug traffickers are disproportionately black or Hispanic, the police don't need to be racist to stop many minority motorists; they simply have to be efficient in targeting potential drug traffickers. It is an unfortunate fact that much higher proportions of black children than white grow up at a social disadvantage and are more tempted to break society's rules. Thus, although blacks are only 12% of the American population, in a recent year they comprised 56% of the arrests for murder, 42% of the arrests for rape, 61% of the arrests for robbery, 39% of the arrests for aggravated assault, 31% of the arrests for burglary, 33% of the arrests for larceny and 40% of the arrests for motor vehicle theft. Also 46% of state prison inmates—i.e., those actually convicted of crimes—were black (another 17% were Hispanic). Why should they not be equally overrepresented in drug trafficking, which is less easy to measure statistically?

Some police officers are no doubt racists and some are guilty of misconduct. But it is dangerous to make public policy on the basis of such horrible examples as the Amadou Diallo shooting. All professionals make mistakes: Surgeons operate on the wrong kidney; lawyers botch cross-examinations. Fairness requires that mistakes be looked at in the context of the more numerous examples of good judgment.

House Calls

But the police deserve extra leeway for their mistakes because, unlike other professionals, they don't have the luxury of turning down unpleasant cases. They make house calls despite personal danger. They have to deal with not only criminals but also paranoid schizophrenics who have not taken their medication or suicidal people. The police come and do their best because the buck stops with them. Usually they succeed; occasionally, and sometimes tragically, they fail.

So should the New York City Police Department be convicted of racism? And should Mr. Williams have been fired as superintendent of the New Jersey State Police? Not in my opinion. True, the police in the Diallo case should have used better judgment, and Mr. Williams could have tiptoed more gently over the unpleasant reality that interdicting drug shipments on the New Jersey Turnpike requires stopping more black than white motorists. But he was defending his officers against what he considered a bum rap: that they were racists. By a wide margin, they are not.

Periodical Bibliography

The following articles have been selected to supplement the diverse views presented in this chapter. Addresses are provided for periodicals not indexed in the *Readers' Guide to Periodical Literature*, the *Alternative Press Index*, the *Social Sciences Index*, or the *Index to Legal Periodicals and Books*.

Alexander Cockburn	"Free Radio, Crazy Cops, and Broken Windows," *Nation*, December 15, 1997.
William D. Eggers and John O'Leary	"The Beat Generation," *Policy Review*, Fall 1995.
Jan Golab	"Probable Cause," *Los Angeles Magazine*, August 1999.
Rob Gurwitt	"Cops and Community," *Governing*, May 1995.
Sidney L. Harring and Gerda W. Ray	"Policing a Class Society: New York City in the 1990s," *Social Justice*, Summer 1999.
George Kelling	"Policing Under Fire," *Wall Street Journal*, March 23, 1999.
Joy Bennett Kinnon	"DWB: Driving While Black," *Ebony*, September 1999.
Suzanne B. Laparte	"Download Your Local Sheriff," *Policy Review*, March/April 1997.
Joseph D. McNamara	"A Veteran Chief: Too Many Cops Think It's a War," *Time*, September 1, 1997.
Barbara Reynolds	"Our Sons Under Siege," *Essence*, November 1999.
Christopher Swope	"The Electronic Posse," *Governing*, March 1996.
James Traub	"New York Story," *New Republic*, January 27, 1997.
Jodi Wilgoren	"Police Profiling Debate: Acting on Experience, or on Bias," *New York Times*, April 9, 1999.
Gordon Witkin	"Changing the Idea of Law and Order," *U.S. News & World Report*, November 27, 1995.
Richard Wolkomir	"Protect and Serve," *Smithsonian*, November 1998.

CHAPTER 4

Who Should Police the Police?

Chapter Preface

Police have been reading suspects their rights—the right to remain silent and the right to an attorney—since 1966 when the Supreme Court ruled that suspects' confessions were inadmissible in court if the suspects had not been advised of their rights. The Miranda rule was a way to rein in officers who were so eager to get convictions for suspects that they used abusive means to obtain questionable confessions. The Court viewed the Miranda warning as a way to police the police and protect suspects' rights, but the rule is now at the center of an intense legal debate about whether the rule handcuffs police and allows the guilty to go free.

Opponents of the Miranda rule argue that the courts are forced to set many criminals free because police failed to properly advise suspects of their rights. Paul Cassell, a legal scholar at the University of Utah and the most vocal opponent of the Miranda warning, argues that "a perfectly guilty murderer can go free because of a technical argument." He calls the Miranda rule "the most damaging blow to law enforcement in 50 years."

Those who favor keeping the Miranda rule argue that the warning protects the rights of those arrested and interrogated by the police and reduces police brutality by reminding officers that suspects have rights. They maintain that the Miranda warning eliminates forced and dishonest confessions because it informs suspects that they do not need to speak to police without an attorney present. Furthermore, supporters contend that few suspects are freed because police failed to read the Miranda warning to them. As Laurence A. Benner, professor of constitutional law at California Western School of Law, argues, "facts show that Miranda has had little impact on the ability of police to acquire sufficient information to convict."

The Miranda rule was originally conceived as a way to protect suspects' rights and to keep police accountable for treating suspects fairly. Many accountability systems have been tried in attempts to police the police. The authors in the following chapter weigh the strengths and weaknesses of some of those efforts to monitor police conduct.

VIEWPOINT

1

"Without effective civilian controls, 'broken-windows policing' is just broken-kneecaps policing."

Civilian Oversight Reduces Police Brutality

Nation

In the following viewpoint, the *Nation* argues that police brutality is a serious civil rights problem because police departments rarely discipline offending officers. Furthermore, the *Nation* asserts that the threat of expensive misconduct lawsuits does not provide police departments with an incentive to reform because cities pay for the suits, not police departments. Without effective civilian review boards to monitor police brutality, the magazine maintains that abuse will flourish because no other accountability system exists within police departments to curb it. The *Nation* is a weekly magazine covering political and cultural issues.

As you read, consider the following questions:
1. Why did New York police kill Gidone Busch, according to the *Nation*?
2. According to the magazine, what percentage of the officers charged with brutality had a history of misconduct?
3. What was the average cost per year to the city of Los Angeles to settle misconduct settlements in the period between 1991 to 1996, according to the *Nation*?

Reprinted from "Broken-Kneecap Policing," editorial, *The Nation*, October 11, 1999, by permission of *The Nation*.

"**I** think the knee-jerk reaction of attacking the police has gone way too far in this city." Thus spake New York's Mayor Rudolph Giuliani. This after officers pumped twelve fatal rounds into Gidone Busch in 1999, a disturbed Orthodox Jew wielding a hammer ("a claw hammer," the mayor and police chief echoed, to make that ordinary household object sound as sinister as possible).

Broken-Kneecaps Policing

Abusive policing remains the nation's most visible civil rights crisis. Two articles in the October 11, 1999, issue of *Nation*, by actor Alton Fitzgerald White of Broadway's *Ragtime* and David Cole [who writes for *The Nation*], expose how police racism is countenanced in the court system and in the precinct house. But as Gidone Busch's death makes clear, the problem is not racism alone. Rather, the presumption of guilt embedded in racial profiling becomes even more insidious and incendiary when it is backed up by a police lobby so powerful that officers know they will never be called to account.

Abusive law enforcement, hardly a new problem, has risen to crisis proportions because "modernization" of policing has far outpaced police accountability. Police have more of everything than they had ten years ago: more money and officers; a whole new toolbelt, from more sophisticated computer crime-mapping to more lethal sidearms; new theories of crime control. But they have the old system for dealing with problems and public complaints: the cover-up. Without effective civilian controls, "broken-windows policing" is just broken-kneecaps policing with a PhD.

New York City is a case in point. Public Advocate Mark Green, the mayor's *bête noire*, recently unveiled a study showing that of 283 cases of police misconduct deemed worthy of action by the city's Civilian Complaint Review Board, the department filed charges in only a third. Just as important, Green found that 73 percent of the officers cited in those complaints had a history of misconduct, showing on the one hand just how tolerant the NYPD bureaucracy is of abusive policing, and on the other that misconduct, far from inevitable, resides in a core of troubled officers.

Police Abuse Costs Money

Lawsuits against abusive officers and departments are costing taxpayers a bundle. Under Giuliani, New York taxpayers have gone from paying $14.6 million in police misconduct settlements in 1994 to forking over $31.2 million in 1998. Detroit's police misconduct cases between July 1995 and April 1997 cost an average of $10 million per year, while Los Angeles's payout averaged $13.2 million per year over a six-year period ending in 1996. But as an incentive for police reform these lawsuits are meaningless: In New York, Detroit and Los Angeles—along with Philadelphia and Chicago—not one dime for lawless policing comes from police budgets. San Francisco is the only exception. In 1996 the city enacted a law requiring that the police budget pay for police abuses. The results have been salutary: From 1996 to 1998 the city spent just $2.6 million per year on all claims, not just misconduct.

Reprinted by permission of Mickey Siporin.

Politicians from President Bill Clinton to New Jersey Governor Christine Todd Whitman have tried to mollify public concern about policing by denouncing racial profiling. But few of them have proposed reining in police with systematic reform. Neither has Attorney General Janet Reno.

Her civil rights division has filed some effective high-profile lawsuits against police departments, and in 1999 the Justice Department finally began collecting data on racial profiling. But Reno has declined to endorse a national commitment to meaningful civilian oversight boards, the only mechanism for public control of police. This cries out for Congressional action. It's time to cut off federal funding to any police department without an effective accountability system. Without radical reform, lawless law enforcement will grow.

"*[Civilian review boards] generally help the police supervise the community more than they help the community supervise the police.*"

Civilian Oversight Does Not Prevent Police Brutality

Ken Boettcher

Ken Boettcher argues in the following viewpoint that civilian review boards designed to monitor and curb police abuse do not prevent police brutality. Boettcher maintains that civilian review boards are ineffective because they have little disciplinary and investigative power. Furthermore, the author contends that brutality and racism against the poor and minorities are inherent in the role of police, which is to aggressively defend the interests of the wealthy. Boettcher writes for the *People*, a socialist newspaper.

As you read, consider the following questions:
1. How many police departments were being policed by citizen review boards in 1997, according to Boettcher?
2. According to Amnesty International, how many of the victims of police brutality are racial minorities?
3. In the author's opinion, what objective should workers strive for to reduce police brutality?

Reprinted from "Why 'Civilian Review Boards' Can't End Police Brutality," by Ken Boettcher, *The People*, June 1998, by permission of the Socialist Labor Party.

Under the headline "Weak Powers, Resources Make Job Tough for Police Watchdogs," an Associated Press news brief observed that "American cities large and small are launching a second generation of civilian police oversight boards despite critics' complaints that the first group of watchdog panels has been largely powerless to investigate or discipline police."

As of 1997, there were at least 102 police departments across the nation that were ostensibly being "policed" by civilian review boards or something like them by a different name. These boards are an outgrowth of complaints about police brutality and violence.

Police Are Inherently Brutal

While the agitation for such reform seems to come in "waves," hostilities between police and the communities they supposedly "serve" are bound to be constant—though they are often only noted in the major media when some high-profile victim suffers, or a particularly outrageous example of police brutality occurs.

Brutality is inherent in the social role of the police. The police, being an instrument of force, are nothing but the armed wing of the capitalist state at the local level. As such, their primary functions are to defend capitalist property and political interests, and to maintain social order on ruling-class terms.

Defense of capitalist property and political interests often entails the use of physical force to keep down the ruled class, as evidenced by the frequent use of the police against strikes and demonstrations. The maintenance of order in a system that breeds discontent can only fuel the brutal character of the police; and insofar as capitalist discrimination keeps minorities heavily concentrated among the more destitute, desperate and demoralized elements of the working class, racial and other prejudices readily take root among the police.

Civilian Review Is Powerless

Brutality and prejudice are further reinforced by the ruling class' strident calls for "getting tough" or "cracking down" on working-class crime and other signs of social breakdown and demoralization. They are still further reinforced by a kind of military subculture that exists among most police forces that promotes authoritarianism and aggression, and that frequently condones racist speech and viewpoints.

Citizen Review Boards Cover Up Brutality

The work of the New York City CCRB [Civilian Complaint Review Board] comes down to this: The many thousands of people each year who are subjected to police harassment, cursing, insults, racial slurs, beatings, trumped-up charges and false arrests are told to file official complaints. Often the police try to intimidate or talk people out of filing complaints. When complaints are filed, they are usually officially dismissed. The cases that do not get immediately dropped by the CCRB are dismissed by the Police Commissioner, with a very few exceptions. And these few exceptions almost always end up with token "punishment" of the cops.

This is a process that serves to cover up the systematic brutality of the NYPD, rather than helping the victims of police abuse. The workings of the CCRB actually shed more light on the ugly epidemic of police brutality raging in New York City.

Revolutionary Worker, November 15, 1998.

In New York, where Mayor Rudolph Giuliani's get-tough "Zero Tolerance" program has targeted minor offenders, police violence is on the rise despite its civilian review board. As a 1996 Amnesty International report observed, "Reports of police brutality, shootings and deaths in police custody in New York City have risen significantly in recent years, with more than two-thirds of the victims belonging to racial minorities."

The trend, nationwide, is similar—hence the renewed effort to establish, or reestablish on a better footing, civilian review boards. That such boards have not been effective is hardly surprising. As a 1997 article in *Time* magazine observed, "Many [civilian review boards] have no subpoena power and meager investigative staff, which leaves them powerless to get to the bottom of cases. While the New York board is supposed to be made up entirely of citizens, a majority of its members are former law enforcement officials, prosecutors and lawyers."

Police Exist to Repress Unrest

It might seem that a police force could be cured of brutality and prejudice if it was truly under the control of, and responsible to, all the people of a community. That is the sentiment that prompts popular pressure, where it exists, for civilian review boards.

However, the record shows that many such boards effectively co-opt citizen demands without doing anything to rein in police violence. They generally help the police supervise the community more than they help the community supervise the police.

Undoubtedly there are individual cases where such programs may have helped ease tensions and reduced the level or frequency of police brutality, but they cannot eliminate the root of the problem.

The creation of a "gentler and kinder" police force is an impossible social objective. The police can never be transformed into a humane institution, whether by investigations, disciplinary action or "better supervision." The most that such things can accomplish is to create dangerous illusions for the working class. Ultimately, the police exist because repression is the political state's final answer to the growing social strife bred by the disintegrating capitalist system.

The objective workers should strive for is the creation of a society in which there would be no need to maintain order by brute force. A socialist society would be a self-governing, classless society of free and equal producers in which, the class-based economic cause of social discontent, deprivation and demoralization having been uprooted, there would be no subordinate class to hold down.

> "[The white wall of silence] is why many
> law-abiding members of minority groups
> are convinced they have more to fear from
> cops . . . than they do from common
> criminals."

Codes of Silence Prevent Effective Oversight

Jack E. White

Jack E. White argues in the following viewpoint that cover-ups of wrongdoing within police departments are tolerated by white citizens who do not care what police do so long as they are directed against others and protect their own interests. This "white wall of silence," he contends, ensures the existence of the "blue wall of silence"—a term used to describe the reluctance of police officers to report misconduct by fellow officers. White maintains that these codes of silence act as bulwarks that prevent those concerned about police brutality from effectively monitoring officer conduct. Only high-profile and unusually brutal attacks, the author asserts, provoke officers to break the code of silence and inform on one another. White writes for *Time* magazine.

As you read, consider the following questions:
1. What did officer Volpe do to Abner Louima in August 1997, according to White?
2. According to the author, what should the blue wall of silence be called?
3. Why did police shoot Margaret L. Mitchell in May 1999, according to the author?

Reprinted from "The White Wall of Silence," by Jack E. White, *Time*, June 7, 1999, by permission of Time-Life Syndications. Copyright ©1999 Time Inc.

Suppose that on one fateful night in August 1997, New York City cop Justin Volpe had contented himself with pummeling Abner Louima with his nightstick instead of ramming a broom handle into Louima's rectum and then waving it in front of his face. Suppose that after that vicious assault, Volpe had not pranced around the precinct house with the blood-and-feces-stained stick, inviting other cops to examine it. And suppose the victim had not made the headline-grabbing (though phony) allegation that his tormentors had exulted, "This is Giuliani time!"—a reference to the city's tough-talking Mayor Rudolph Giuliani. There would be a good chance that we would never have heard of Louima and that Volpe would still be patrolling his beat in Brooklyn. Instead Volpe, 27, pleaded guilty in May 1997 in federal court to an act of police brutality so sadistic that it cracked "the blue wall of silence."

The Blue Wall of Silence

That is the high-sounding euphemism that New York's Finest use for their ingrained habit of refusing to "rat" about misconduct by fellow officers. They ought to call it just obstruction of justice, so ruthlessly enforced by ostracism and even bodily harm that only a few officers have the guts and integrity to break ranks when misconduct occurs. But the assault on Louima was so savage that Volpe's fellow cops could not tolerate it. Detective Eric Turetzky testified that he saw Volpe lead Louima, in handcuffs and with his pants around his ankles, away from the bathroom area where the incident occurred. Officer Mark Schofield said that when Volpe returned a pair of leather gloves he had borrowed before the assault, they were stained with blood. Sergeant Kenneth Wernick said Volpe had bragged to him that "I took a man down tonight" before showing him the stick he had used.

Faced with this evidence, Volpe pleaded guilty to six federal charges, in the hope of avoiding the maximum sentence of life in prison. (Four other cops were accused in the attack; [one, Charles Schwarz, was found guilty, and the three others were acquitted].) "If you tell anybody about this, I'll find you and kill you," Volpe admitted warning Louima that night. But, tellingly, while Volpe apologized "for hurting my

WHITE AMERICA DISCOVERS POLICE BRUTALITY...

WHITE AMERICA DOES SOMETHING ABOUT IT...

⁂CLICK⁂

Marlette ©1991 Newsday. Distributed by Los Angeles Times Syndicate. Reprinted with permission.

family," he offered no apology to his victim. Nor was there any apology from Volpe's lawyer, Marvyn Kornberg, who had claimed—without evidence—that the ruptured bladder and rectal lacerations that Louima, a married father of two, had suffered in the attack were the result of consensual gay sex.

The White Wall of Silence

But does Volpe's guilty plea mean that the blue wall of silence is finally tumbling down, as Giuliani and Police Commissioner Howard Safir claim? Don't bet on it. Several law-enforcement experts told *Time* correspondent Elaine Rivera that they believe the code of silence remains intact. Volpe refused to name other officers who took part in the assault. And the officers who testified against him waited days and weeks to come forward—and did so then only under the pressure of a highly publicized investigation. Says New York City police lieutenant Eric Adams, co-founder of One Hundred Blacks in Law Enforcement Who Care [a New York City Police Department discrimination watchdog group]: "If a civilian were to see another civilian sodomize a person and wait days or weeks to say anything, that could be considered a major crime."

But there is a deeper reason that the Louima case doesn't

necessarily portend a slowdown in attempts to cover up police brutality. Call it the white wall of silence—the implicit bargain that Giuliani, like the mayors of many cities, has made with his mostly white core political supporters. They reckon that voters will tolerate heavy-handed police tactics as long as they don't have to see them; that most nonwhites, especially young males, are considered suspect, and that wholesale violations of their civil liberties are an acceptable price to pay for a drop in the crime rate. That is why police brutality is an explosive issue from New York to Los Angeles, where protests broke out in May 1999 after police shot and killed Margaret L. Mitchell, a college-educated black woman who had been homeless since developing a mental illness, after she reportedly lunged at them with a screwdriver. It is why the street-crimes unit in New York—four of whose members are charged with murder in the [1999] shooting of Amadou Diallo, an unarmed African street merchant—have stopped and frisked thousands of blacks and Hispanics for no reason except their color. It is why many law-abiding members of minority groups are convinced they have more to fear from cops like Volpe than they do from common criminals. Until the white majority makes it clear that it will not tolerate such abuses, they are bound to go on.

"[The blue wall of silence] was never really the mighty barrier it had been cracked up to be."

The Police Code of Silence Is Exaggerated

James Lardner

In the following viewpoint, James Lardner contends that "the blue wall of silence"—a term used to describe police officers' refusal to inform on one another—is exaggerated. He asserts that police officers have a long history of reporting abuse by fellow officers. In addition, Lardner maintains that today's more diverse police departments may undermine the historic loyalties that may have discouraged officers from exposing one another's misconduct in the past. Lardner writes for *U.S. News & World Report*.

As you read, consider the following questions:
1. What boast did Officer Justin Volpe make to fellow officers, according to Lardner?
2. According to the author, what did Officer Cairnes do in 1857 that provoked a fellow officer to inform on him?
3. In the author's view, what consequences did Eric Turetsky and Mark Schofield experience as a result of informing on a fellow officer?

In October of 1997 [a new police picture has] drawn widespread attention. In the movie *Cop Land*, the dream of affordable housing and an easy commute across the George Washington Bridge leads a precinctful of New York City cops to sell out to the mob and wreak murder and mayhem across upper Manhattan and northern New Jersey. Meanwhile, in a Brooklyn hospital in October 1997, a Haitian immigrant was lucky to be alive after what a federal prosecutor called "an almost incomprehensible act of depravity" allegedly inflicted upon him by representatives of the selfsame New York City Police Department [NYPD].

Anything Goes

The Brooklyn case presents a challenge for Mayor Rudolph Giuliani, whose popularity has rested, more than anything, on New Yorkers' belief that he has crime—and the police—under control. But the timing may be propitious for *Cop Land*, which could easily have been dismissed as well-acted nonsense instead of being hailed for its gritty authenticity. Could any band of cops really be as amoral and cocksure as the one led by Harvey Keitel in this movie? Writer-director James Mangold can now point skeptics toward the 70th Precinct, where patrolman Justin Volpe is accused of using a toilet-plunger stick to sodomize—and very nearly kill—a man who may or may not have struck him in a scuffle outside a Flatbush nightclub. After exacting his revenge, Volpe allegedly boasted to coworkers that he had found it necessary to "bring a man down tonight." This incident could suggest that the NYPD, like *Cop Land*, is a place where some people think they can get away with anything.

Beyond this point, though, the two plots diverge. In the fictional 37th Precinct of *Cop Land*, the hallowed "blue wall of silence" stands well-nigh impregnable, and it falls to a mousy suburban sheriff (played, in a career rethink, by Sylvester Stallone) to expose the conspiracy. In the real 70th Precinct, a number of cops were reportedly troubled at the outset by their glimpses of what had occurred, and as they got wind of its full horror, according to investigators, several of them were driven to come forward.

Truth or lore? How to explain this strange behavior,

which goes so directly against everything the entertainment industry has taught us about the police? A law enforcement source told the [New York] *Daily News* that history had been made: The blue wall of silence, like the Berlin Wall, had fallen. Maybe, though, it was never really the mighty barrier it had been cracked up to be.

Cops Do Blow the Whistle

In scandals going back more than a century, New York City cops have, in fact, given evidence against other cops. In 1857, the first year that the force had handguns, the testimony of an outraged colleague led to the arrest of a certain Officer Cairnes in the fatal shooting of a certain Sailor Jack—an Irish immigrant who tried to flee after being arrested for disorderly conduct. "What did you do that for? You had plenty of help!" the accusing cop was said to have exclaimed.

Code of Silence Is Shattered

For some observers . . . high-profile testimony [by police officers exposing the wrongdoing of other officers] heralds a breakthough in police behavior and dramatic proof that the stubborn code of silence—immortalized in *Serpico*, *Prince of the City* and other movies about police corruption—has been pierced. "All of [the officers who testified against New York City officer Justin Volpe, accused of sodomizing Abner Louima in 1997,] did the right thing, the courageous thing in deciding to come forward, and this kind of testimony happens much more often than people have been led to believe," New York Police Commissioner Howard Safir said in an interview.

Josh Getlin, *Los Angeles Times*, May 22, 1999.

Not infrequently, cops have tried to blow the whistle, only to discover that no one in authority cared to listen. This was the prolonged experience of [NYPD] Detective David Durk and Patrolman Frank Serpico, who precipitated the Knapp Commission investigation of the early 1970s. [Durk and Serpico testified against fellow officers at hearings on police corruption, and the Knapp Commission was established to investigate abuse on the force.] The pattern repeated itself when, in the late 1980s, members of the force repeatedly tried to get action taken against [NYPD] Patrolman Michael Dowd and his "crew" of drug-dealing cops—a case finally broken, a la *Cop Land*, by local authorities in the suburban jurisdictions where several of the cops lived.

In *Cop Land*, as in popular lore, there is loyalty and there is rathood, and the mere suspicion of the latter is enough to get a cop killed. Whistle-blowing was never quite as suicidal as this, and the police profession has grown a lot less insular than it used to be. Step into just about any precinct, and you will find women, minorities, college graduates, budding screenwriters, and all manner of other characters who can't necessarily be trusted to keep their mouths shut.

News accounts of the 70th Precinct case in October 1997 contained the names of two cops, Eric Turetzky and Mark Schofield, who had given evidence. At last report, they were alive, on duty, and being saluted by friends, family, the mayor, the police commissioner, and at least some of their peers. Perhaps it is not even a stretch to imagine that, in a case as grotesque as this, coming forward will be easier for them to explain in the long run than holding back would be. Only Hollywood, I suspect, will have any trouble with that.

Periodical Bibliography

The following articles have been selected to supplement the diverse views presented in this chapter. Addresses are provided for periodicals not indexed in the *Readers' Guide to Periodical Literature*, the *Alternative Press Index*, the *Social Sciences Index*, or the *Index to Legal Periodicals and Books*.

David Barstow	"Police Wall of Silence Shows Some Cracks in Torture Case," *New York Times*, May 21, 1999.
Angela Bonavoglia	"Breaking the Blue Wall of Silence," *Ms.*, January/February 1997.
Kevin Flynn	"Civilian Complaints Said to Be Slighted by New York Police," *New York Times*, September 15, 1999.
Josh Getlin	"NYPD Brutality Testimony Spotlights Code of Silence," *Los Angeles Times*, May 22, 1999. Available from Times Mirror Square, Los Angeles, CA 90053.
Elizabeth Gleick	"The Crooked Blue Line," *Time*, September 11, 1995.
David Kocieniewski	"System of Policing the Police Is Attacked from Without and Within," *New York Times*, December 19, 1997.
Jack Maple	"Police Must Be Held Accountable," *Newsweek*, June 21, 1999.
Newsweek	"Justice for Louima," June 7, 1999.
Revolutionary Worker	"If You Dare to Complain About Police Abuse . . ." November 15, 1998. Available from Box 3486, Merchandise Mart, Chicago, IL 60654.
Ann Scott Tyson	"Moves to Police the Police Gain Ground," *Christian Science Monitor*, November 13, 1996.
Lynne Wilson	"Cops vs. Citizen Review," *Covert Action Quarterly*, Winter 1995–1996.

For Further Discussion

Chapter 1

1. Arch Puddington claims that statistics on police brutality are not compiled, yet both he and Human Rights Watch come to conclusions about the extent of police brutality. What evidence does each viewpoint use to support its argument about the prevalence of brutality, and which author do you think makes the more convincing case? Explain your answer.

2. Sunil Dutta comes to the conclusion that the police are not corrupt by generalizing from his personal experience, while Joseph D. McNamara concludes that police corruption is widespread by generalizing from media accounts of individually corrupt officers. In your opinion, which do you believe is the most reliable method of forming conclusions, generalizing from personal observation or from media accounts? Explain your answer by outlining the strengths and weaknesses of both methods.

3. Both Oliver "Buck" Revell and Phyllis Schlafly draw conclusions about the FBI based on one event, the Waco siege. In your opinion, does the FBI's handling of this one high-profile case provide enough evidence from which to form arguments about the competence and reliability of the FBI? What other information might help you evaluate the FBI in the Waco case and generally? Explain your answer.

Chapter 2

1. Salim Muwakkil cites several examples of police brutality to support his argument that the police are racist. Michael Levin supports his argument that the police are not racist by citing statistics that show blacks commit more violent crimes than whites. In your opinion, do both authors reason from the facts correctly? That is, without knowing whether or not the police shootings that Muwakkil describes were justified, can you ascertain for sure that the police were motivated by racism? Do the statistics Levin cites prove that more blacks become criminals or only that they are apprehended more often than whites? Explain which author makes a better argument and why.

2. In arguing for better police training in the handling of the mentally ill, the *Los Angeles Times* states that loose animals in the city are sometimes treated with more consideration than mentally ill suspects. In your opinion, what kind of attitude should the police have toward people suspected of criminal be-

havior? Respect? Anger? Should the police punish or protect? Explain your answer and tell why you believe as you do.

3. Tracy Fitzsimmons maintains that female officers do a better job than male officers at diffusing potentially violent situations and therefore reduce police brutality. In your opinion, what qualities do effective police officers have? Do you think both men and women possess these qualities or are the qualities you name innate to one gender or the other? Explain your answer.

Chapter 3

1. Mona Charen argues that assertive policing in New York City has lowered crime rates and has not increased the number of police brutality cases. Clarence Page maintains that New York City's assertive policing has led to an increase in civil rights violations and police use of excessive force. Is a reduction of one hundred police shootings in one year proof that brutality has declined? Or does an increase in civilian complaints against the police prove that brutality is on the rise? Which author constructs a better argument and why?

2. Edmund F. McGarrell contends that community policing helps reduce crime by encouraging police officers to work with neighborhood residents to prevent crime before it can happen. The *Revolutionary Worker* argues that the police can never be trusted because they represent the power structure that oppresses the poor living in crime-ridden neighborhoods. McGarrell is a well-educated professional working at a large government institution. The *Revolutionary Worker*, claiming to be the voice of the common people, is a communist newspaper opposed to democratic institutions. In your opinion, which author is more qualified to draw conclusions about community policing and why?

3. Jackson Toby argues that racial profiling is effective because it allows police to focus on those who are most likely to commit crimes. Bob Herbert claims that racial profiling is unjust because it targets many more innocent people than guilty ones. If it is true that more blacks than whites engage in drug trafficking, and if it is true that stopping them more often reduces crime, do you think police are justified in using race as a basis for stopping motorists? Explain your answer.

Chapter 4

1. The *Nation* argues that effective citizen review boards can reduce cases of police brutality by targeting the few officers who are abusive. Ken Boettcher contends that citizen review boards

cannot reduce police brutality because it is systematic and inherent in the social role of the police. What evidence does the *Nation* use to support its argument that abuse is restricted to a few officers? What evidence does Boettcher cite to support his conclusion that police abuse is systematic? In your opinion, which author makes the more convincing argument and why?

2. Jack E. White argues that police officers rarely report cases of abuse by a fellow officer and that this "code of silence" is tolerated by white citizens who support the police no matter what so long as their interests are protected. James Lardner maintains that the "code of silence" has been broken more often than people think and will be broken more in the future as police departments diversify. What are the pros and cons of such internal loyalty? List other examples of groups whose members tend to protect each other from outside interference. Do these other examples of the code of silence serve the same purpose and create the same kinds of problems as the "blue wall of silence"?

Organizations to Contact

The editors have compiled the following list of organizations concerned with the issues debated in this book. The descriptions are derived from materials provided by the organizations. All have publications or information available for interested readers. The list was compiled on the date of publication of the present volume; the information provided here may change. Be aware that many organizations take several weeks or longer to respond to inquiries, so allow as much time as possible.

American Civil Liberties Union (ACLU)
125 Broad St., 15th Floor, New York, NY 10004-2400
website: www.aclu.org

The ACLU is a national organization that works to defend Americans' civil rights guaranteed in the U.S. Constitution. Among other services, the ACLU provides legal assistance to victims of police abuse. The ACLU publishes *Fighting Police Abuse: A Community Action Manual* as well as the semiannual newsletter *Civil Liberties Alert*.

Amnesty International (AI)
322 Eighth Ave., New York, NY 10001
(212) 807-8400 • fax: (212) 627-1451
e-mail: ai@aiusa.org • website: www.amnesty.org

Amnesty International is a worldwide campaigning movement that works to promote human rights and opposes cruel treatment of prisoners. Its report *Police Brutality and Excessive Force in the New York City Police Department* is available on the AI website.

The Heritage Foundation
214 Massachusetts Ave. NE, Washington, DC 20002-4999
(202) 546-4400 • fax: (202) 546-8328
e-mail: info@heritage.org • website: www.heritage.org

The Heritage Foundation is a conservative public policy research institute that advocates strengthening law enforcement to stop crime. It publishes position papers on a broad range of topics, including police issues. Its regular publications include the monthly *Policy Review*, the *Backgrounder* series of occasional papers, and the Heritage Lecture series.

Human Rights Watch
350 Fifth Ave., 34th Floor, New York, NY 10118-3299
(212) 290-4700 • fax: (212) 736-1300
e-mail: hrwnyc@hrw.org • website: www.hrw.org

Human Rights Watch monitors and reports human rights abuses in the United States and internationally. It sponsors fact-finding missions, disseminates results, and publishes the bimonthly *Human Rights Watch* newsletter.

International Association of Women Police (IAWP)
RR#1, Box 149, Deer Isle, ME 04627
e-mail: iawp@iawp.org • website: http://iawp.org

The IAWP envisions a world where women working in the criminal justice professions are treated justly, fairly, and equitably by the agencies they serve. The association provides network and support systems, training, and information aimed at increasing awareness and encouraging women to enter the criminal justice field. The organization publishes *Women Police* magazine.

The John Howard Society of Canada
771 Montreal St., Kingston, ON K7K 3J6 Canada
(613) 542-7547 • fax: (613) 542-6824
e-mail: national@johnhoward.ca • website: http://johnhoward.ca

The mission of the John Howard Society is to aid in the effective, just, and humane response to the causes and consequences of crime. It provides advocacy, research, education, and communication in its efforts to promote its goals.

National Association for the Advancement of Colored People (NAACP)
1025 Vermont Ave. NW, Suite 1120, Washington, DC 20005
(202) 638-2269
website: www.naacp.org

The NAACP is a civil rights organization that works to end racial discrimination in America. It researches and documents police brutality and provides legal services for victims of brutality. The NAACP publishes the book *Beyond the Rodney King Story: An Investigation of Police Misconduct in Minority Communities*, the magazine *Crisis* ten times per year, and *Police-Citizen Violence: An Organizing Guide for Community Leaders*, which is available from its civil rights archives.

National Black Police Association (NBPA)

3251 Mt. Pleasant St. NW, 2nd Floor, Washington, DC 20010-2103
(202) 986-2070 • fax: (202) 986-0410
e-mail: NBPANATOFC@ world.att.net
website: www.blackpolice.org

The association is a nationwide organization of African American police associations dedicated to the promotion of justice, fairness, and effectiveness in law enforcement. The NBPA serves as an advocate for minority police officers.

National Coalition on Police Accountability (N-COPA)

59 East Van Buren, Suite 2418, Chicago, IL 60605
(312) 663-5392 • fax: (312) 663-5396
e-mail: nkrhodes@mailbox.syr.edu • website: http://web.syr.edu

N-COPA is an organization of religious, community, legal groups, and progressive law-enforcement representatives working to hold police accountable to their communities through public education, community organization, legislation, litigation, and promotion of empowered independent oversight.

Police Executive Research Forum (PERF)

1120 Connecticut Ave. NW, Suite 930, Washington, DC 20036
(202) 466-7820 • fax: (202) 466-7826
website: www.policeforum.org

PERF is a national professional association of police executives that seeks to increase public understanding of and stimulate debate on important criminal justice issues. PERF's numerous publications include the books *And Justice for All: Understanding and Controlling Police Abuse of Force* and the papers *The Force Factor: Measuring Police Use of Force Relative to Suspect Resistance* and *Police Use of Force: A Statistical Analysis of the Metro-Dade Police Department*.

Police Foundation

2101 Connecticut Ave. NW, Washington, DC 20036
(202) 833-1460 • fax: (202) 659-9149
e-mail: pfinfo@policefoundation.org
website: www.policefoundation.org

The foundation conducts research projects on police activities and aims to improve the quality of police personnel. It publishes the report *Officer Behavior in Police-Citizen Encounters: A Descriptive Model and Implications for Less-than-Lethal Alternatives* and the book *Police Use of Force: Official Reports, Citizen Complaints, and Legal Consequences*.

Bibliography of Books

Amnesty International — *United States of America: Police Brutality and Excessive Force in the New York City Police Department,* June 1996. Available from 322 Eighth Ave., New York, NY 10001.

Janis Appier — *Policing Women: The Sexual Politics of Law Enforcement and the LAPD.* Philadelphia: Temple University Press, 1998.

William J. Bratton with Peter Knobler — *Turnaround: How America's Top Cop Reversed the Crime Epidemic.* New York: Random House, 1998.

Marcia R. Chaiken — *Kids, Cops, and Communities.* Washington, DC: U.S. Department of Justice, 1998.

Paul Chevigny — *Edge of the Knife: Police Violence in the Americas.* New York: New, 1995.

Edwin J. Delattre and Patrick V. Murphy — *Character and Cops: Ethics in Policing.* Washington, DC: American Enterprise Institute for Public Policy Research, 1996.

Norman Dennis, ed. — *Zero Tolerance: Policing a Free Society.* London: IEA Health and Welfare Unit, 1998.

Connie Fletcher — *Breaking and Entering: Women Cops Talk About Life in the Ultimate Men's Club.* New York: HarperCollins, 1995.

Joel Garner — *Understanding the Use of Force by and Against the Police.* Washington, DC: U.S. Department of Justice, 1996.

James C. Howell — *Juvenile Justice and Youth Violence.* Thousand Oaks, CA: Sage, 1997.

Robert Jackall — *Wild Cowboys: Urban Marauders and the Forces of Order.* Cambridge, MA: Harvard University Press, 1997.

George L. Kelling and Catherine M. Coles — *Fixing Broken Windows: Restoring Order and Reducing Crime in Our Communities.* New York: Martin Kessler, 1996.

John Kleinig — *The Ethics of Policing.* Cambridge, MA: Cambridge University Press, 1996.

David B. Kopel and Paul H. Blackman — *No More Wacos: What's Wrong With Federal Law Enforcement and How to Fix It.* New York: Prometheus, 1997.

Rickey D. Lashley — *Policework: The Need for a Noble Character.* Westport, CT: Praeger, 1995.

Susan Ehrlich Martin and Nancy C. Jurik	*Doing Justice, Doing Gender*. Thousand Oaks, CA: Sage, 1996.
Stephen Mastrofski	*Community Policing in Action: Lessons from an Observational Study*. Washington, DC: U.S. Department of Justice, 1998.
Tom McEwen	*National Data Collection on Police Use of Force*. Washington, DC: National Institute of Justice, 1996.
Elijah Muhammad	*Police Brutality*. Atlanta: Secretarius, 1997.
Ngaire Naffine	*Feminism and Criminology*. Philadelphia: Temple University Press, 1996.
National Association for the Advancement of Colored People	*Beyond the Rodney King Story: An Investigation of Police Conduct in Minority Communities*. Boston: Northeastern University Press, 1995.
National Center for Women & Policing	*The Status of Women in Policing: 1998*. Available from 8105 West Third St., Los Angeles, CA 90048.
Dick Reavis	*The Ashes of Waco: An Investigation*. New York: Simon & Schuster, 1995.
Robert Rodriguez	*Justice: A Question of Race*. Tempe, AZ: Bilingual, 1997.
Katheryn K. Russell	*The Color of Crime: Racial Hoaxes, White Fear, Black Protectionism, Police Harassment, and Other Macroaggressions*. New York: New York University Press, 1998.
Joseph F. Sheley and James D. Wright	*In the Line of Fire: Youths, Guns, and Violence in Urban America*. New York: Aldine de Gruyter, 1995.
Jeff Slowikowski and Helen Connelling	*Community Policing and Youth*. Washington, DC: U.S. Department of Justice, 1999.
Irving A. Spergel	*The Youth Gang Problem: A Community Approach*. New York: Oxford University Press, 1995.
James D. Tabor and Eugene U. Gallagher	*Why Waco: Cults and the Battle for Religious Freedom in America*. Berkeley: University of California Press, 1995.
U.S. Department of Justice	*Mental Illness: Police Response*. Washington, DC: Police Executive Forum, 1998.
Ved Varma, ed.	*Violence in Children and Adolescents*. Bristol, PA: Jessica Kingsley, 1997.
Samuel Walker, Cassia Spohn and Miriam DeLone	*The Color of Justice: Race, Ethnicity, and Crime in America*. Belmont, CA: Wadsworth, 1996.

Index